SYAMUK
The Lhasa Newars of Kalimpong and Kathmandu

SYAMUKAPU

The Lhasa Newars of Kalimpong and Kathmandu

D.S. Kansakar Hilker

VAJRA
BOOKS

Published and Distributed by

Vajra Books
Jyatha, Thamel, P.O. Box 21779, Kathmandu, Nepal
Tel.: 977-1-4220562, 4246536
e-mail: vajrabooksktm@gmail.com
www.vajrabookshop.com

First Print 2005
First Reprint 2020

ISBN 99946-644-6-8

Cover design and layout by the author
All photographs from Gyan Jyoti *'s personal collection*
All maps prepared by Hans Hilker

Printed in Nepal

The biographies of
Bhajuratna and Gyan Jyoti Kansakar

Preface

This is the story of Bhajuratna Kansakar, a man who with his great sense of responsibility and through his industriousness, became a very successful merchant. The name and fame of Bhajuratna or Syamukapu (meaning white cap in Tibetan) which he later established for himself, the respect and esteem shown to all associated with these names, deserves to be recorded before all this is lost with the generation that once was closely associated with the man himself.

In recent years much has been written about the period in which Bhajuratna, my grandfather lived in. I now attempt to add my contribution to those published material on the Newar Merchants of Lhasa and Kalimpong, with details as narrated by my father Gyan Jyoti. I hope, that this effort of mine fulfils a deeply cherished wish of my father's.

Bhajuratna started as a small trader in Kalimpong, producing copper and brass household goods for the Tibetan market. Over the years he expanded to importing and exporting musk, yak tail, wool, Rolex watches, cotton and woollen textile and rich Indian brocade. Later, business was carried on by his sons under the name Jyoti Brothers, but the family remained popularly known to all as Syamukapu both in Kalimpong and in Tibet.

The business branched out to handling clearing and forwarding jobs through the Calcutta port, to being mine owners in South India, traders in various fur skin, and in gold. The head office was located at Calcutta, with branches in Kalimpong, Lhasa, Phari, Kathmandu, Bombay, Bhilai and in later years Lucknow and Bangalore.

This book is dedicated to my father, Gyan Jyoti, who passed away in Kathmandu on 23 June 2004 before this work could be completed. My father was also an outstanding person, but in a quiet way. This book includes his life story, as it is not possible to write about Syamukapu without mentioning the contribution made by my father. Certain events involving both my grandfather and my father mentioned in Part I and Part II are sometimes brief repetitions, necessary to maintain the smooth drift of my account.

Bhajuratna was a deeply religious man, he was a great benefactor to Buddhism, and did much to support the Theravadas of Nepal that even today years after his death, he is still remembered by all Theravada monks and nuns of Nepal. He lived at a time when Buddhism was at its lowest in Nepal, and supported the Buddhist monks banished from Nepal by the Rana rulers in 1926 and 1944. Gyan Jyoti his second son, continued the support given by his father, to Buddhism in Nepal. Some people stand out more than the others, and both happened to be just such men. Gyan Jyoti and his father Bhajuratna will go down in the Newar history as men to be remembered for generations.

Deb Shova Kansakar Hilker
December 2005

Table of Contents

Introduction

The Newars

Nepal is a land of extreme geographical and ethnic diversity, with various ethnic groups living in the hill regions of Nepal. Broadly speaking they can be divided into two distinct groups according to their racial and linguistic affinities. The Gorkhas or Parbatias who speak an Indo-Aryan language, Nepali, and the speakers of Tibeto-Burman group of dialects.

The Nepali speakers form roughly 58% (census 1981) of the country's total population. Of the remaining 42% half are divided into the Maithali, Bhojpuri, Abadhi, Bengali and Hindi speakers. The other half, the Tibeto-Burman speakers total about 21% and are divided into numerous exclusive dialect groups, such as the Tamangs, Rais, Gurungs, Sherpas and the Newars with their own cultural traditions. Barring the Newars, the Tibeto-Burman groups have typically strong Mongolian physical characteristics. The Newars stand out quite distinctly, with a high level of cultural achievement, represented by a complex civilisation with an urban bias, mainly concentrated in the Kathmandu valley.

The Newars can be roughly divided into the Hindu Newars and the Buddhist Newars. Although together they constitute approximately only 3% of the total population of the country as a whole, they account for 30% of all university teachers and civil servants, and their representation in commerce and industry may be even higher than this.

Socially, culturally and emotionally, there is a wide gulf between the Newars and the other communities of Nepal. They are peaceful and cheerful in character, very emotional but dislike engaging in physical fights. Their peaceful nature has been regarded by the Gorkhas including other ethnic groups as not being a virtue, and were often scoffed at for their so called timidity. It is on this assumption that till 1950, the Newars were denied employment in the Gorkha army.

In earlier years, every young Gorkha dreamed of joining the army, but if a Newar child was asked the same question, the answer would be to become a trader.

John K. Locke S.J. in his book KARUNAMAYA gives his reasons for the lack of further research on the Newars. "The great complexity of Newar culture deters any scholar whose stay in Nepal is limited to a year or two. And the general misconception that the Newars are a peculiar mixture of Hinduism and Buddhism, peculiar only to Nepal, and therefore of little or no interest to students of Buddhism."

The history of Nepal is in fact the history of the Kathmandu Valley, with the Newars being the remnants of an older Nepal. In the past, Kathmandu was a nation within a nation, whose boundaries were the slopes of the mountains surrounding the Kathmandu Valley. The Newars were its original inhabitants, whose arts and tradition constitute the Nepalese culture where ever Nepal's art and history are referred to.

With the unification of Nepal in 1768–1769 under Prithivi Narayan Shah, the Newars became incorporated into greater Nepal. Today they make up about half of the Kathmandu Valley's almost 600,000 population.

And even today, the valley is still referred to as "Nepal" by the Nepalese hill folks, who still say: "I am off to Nepal" when what they actually mean is they are going to Kathmandu.

Nepal Tibet
A Historical Background

The close relation between Nepal and Tibet dates back some centuries, although over the span of centuries the relationship was at times strained. Understanding this historical connection between these two countries calls for a brief look into Nepal's past

Around the early 7th century A.D. the Lichhavi King of Nepal Amsuvarma (588–643) had his daughter Bhrikuti married to Srong Tsang Gampo, the King of Tibet, and as part of her dowry, a troupe of skilled craftsmen travelled with her to Tibet.

Srong Tsang Gampo a year later also married a Chinese princess Weching (or Beching) in order to maintain a good relation with China. With the help of Weching, Bhrikuti helped to spread Buddhism in Tibet, and as a result of their successful combined efforts Bhrikuti came to be called *Harit Tara* – Green Star, and Weching as *Shwet Tara* – White Star. These two figures or *Taras* are often seen on Buddhist alters on both sides of the Buddha.

Due to their nuptial relation, trade also developed between Nepal, Tibet and China, with Nepali merchants going to China via Tibet and vice versa. King Amsuvarma was highly spoken of by the famous Chinese traveller, Hieun Tsang in his account over Nepal.

In the year 1260, at the time of King Jaya Bhima Dev Malla (reigned 1258–1271), Arniko the famous and skilled artisan of Nepal was sent to Tibet to erect a stupa. He led a team of 80 artists and after completing his work in Tibet, at the request of Kubla Khan (1219–1294) he was sent to Peking where he propagated the Nepali pagoda art into China. Arniko is said to have later enjoyed an influential post in the court of Kubla Khan.

During the period of King Yakshya Malla (1428–1482) there was a set back to the Nepal Tibet relationship. Tibetan districts like Kuti and Kirong were annexed to Nepal, these being the main trade routes to Tibet.

After King Yakshya Malla's death in 1482, the friendly relation was once more restored. A trade treaty was drawn up by which the traders of the Kathmandu Valley were permitted to open business houses in Tibet and also to settle there. It also regulated that all trade between India and Tibet be routed through Nepal. The treaties were renewed from time to time, whereby another treaty gave the Nepali Kings the authority of minting silver coins for Tibet. This arrangement benefited Nepal and caused the inflow of Tibetan gold and silver into Nepal.

A treaty drawn up at the time of King Laxmi Nara Simha Malla (1620–1641) declared that when a Nepali trader died in Tibet childless, the government of Nepal was entitled to his property. If a son was born to a Nepali trader by his Tibetan wife, he would be considered a Nepali subject, but if a daughter was born, she would be a subject of the Tibetan government.

Relations between Nepal and Tibet were often not without friction, resulting in war between the two countries.

With the treaty of Nuwakot signed in 1792 when the Chinese defeated and pushed the Nepalese to Nuwakot, Nepal lost its minting right to China, and all the Tibetan territories annexed by Nepal were restored to Tibet.

The size of the Newar community in Tibet kept changing through the years. A French priest Regis-Evariste Huc in circa 1840 is reported as saying the Newars constituted the largest single foreign group in Lhasa. Daniel Wright, a historian in the latter part of the nineteenth century put down the number of Newars living in Lhasa as three thousand, which seems a bit exaggerated even to the Newars themselves. At the end of the twentieth century, they were less than a hundred.

For centuries, Nepal enjoyed a monopoly trade with Tibet over the traditional trade route from Kathmandu northward, over the Himalayan mountains to Khasa and on to Lhasa. However, this came to a standstill when in 1904, Colonel Francis Younghusband was successful in opening an entry point to Tibet for British India in North East India. In the former little kingdom of Sikkim, embedded between Nepal and Bhutan, near the three country corner of Sikkim, Tibet and Bhutan, are two passes, the Nathu La at a height of 4310m. and Jelep La or the Younghusband Pass, at 4374m. The Newars then opted to use the new entry point for their trade with Lhasa, with many later preferring the Nathu La.

The reader must bear in mind that until 1951, Nepal was a land-locked country, a Forbidden Land for Westerners. Unlike British India, Nepal had no infrastructure connecting Kathmandu to the world outside its borders except for the centuries old foot trails over the mountainous terrain. Everything brought into Kathmandu was carried by troops of porters, the country's main mode of transport. The achievements and trade success of the Lhasa Newars is therefore all the more remarkable.

In the second half of the nineteenth century, the railway system was the backbone of British India. It was a network which united the nation, crossing political, social and cultural barriers. It made possible great advances in trade and travel not only for the Indians, but also for the traders of Nepal.

However, it was not until 1937 that the Nepal Government Railway (NGR), a narrow gauge line was established by the Rana Prime Minister Chandra Sumsher, to run between Raxaul and Amlekgunj.

From Kathmandu, the Newar traders passed through Thankot, the formal checkpoint when leaving or entering Kathmandu, then travelled southward via Bhimphedi, Hetauda, Amlekgunj, then from Birgunj to Raxaul the Indian border, and then on to Siliguri, Darjeeling and Kalimpong. From Kalimpong, where many Lhasa Newars had settled down, the next destination was Gangtok, the capital of Sikkim, then via the 15th Mile over the Nathula Pass to Yatung and finally to Lhasa.

Or instead of taking the Nathula Pass via Gangtok, Newar traders from Kalimpong also entered Tibet by travelling from Algarah to Pedong, past Rhenok over the Jelepla Pass, and then to Yatung. Here in Yatung, they met other traders coming from the Nathula or on their way back to Sikkim.

In contrast to their traditional trade route via Khasa, over Nepal's northern Himalayan border, this was now a much more convenient route for the Newars, as much of the goods required by the traders for Tibet were bought in Calcutta, and they were now much easier to transport to Kalimpong.

The Tibet trade via Kalimpong flourished for the Lhasa Newars for over fifty years, but all this changed with the Chinese invasion of Tibet in 1959. And it came to a final stop with the China India war of 1962. This was also the period when most of the Lhasa Newars left Kalimpong for good, and returned to Kathmandu.

Kalimpong and Darjeeling

Before the turn of the 20th century Newar merchants and handworkers such as gold and silver smiths, copper and brass smiths were already well established and prosperous business families in Darjeeling, Ghoom, Kalimpong and Gangtok, and a handful even in Calcutta. As far as anybody can remember, the Newars were also established merchants and craftsmen in Lhasa for generations. Their forefathers being the craftsmen who accompanied Princess Bhrikuti to Tibet in the seventh century. For the Newar traders, the new route via Nathula Pass was convenient, which resulted in more Newar traders establishing settlements in Kalimpong, by buying property and bringing along their families from Kathmandu.

Kalimpong was once the Headquarters of the Bhutanese Government, and was part of Bhutan until 1865. This explains the existence of Bhutan House in Kalimpong, the residence of the Bhutanese royal family, and the home of the Queen Mother. After the Anglo Bhutan war, it was emerged with Darjeeling, became a sub-division of Darjeeling in 1916 and was developed as a hill station. The word Kalim means king's minister, Pong means stronghold.

Darjeeling 2134 m. and Kalimpong 1250 m. above sea level are separated by the Teesta river and two hours by car over a 51 km. long motorable road. They were during the British Raj summer resorts for the Britishers. Other famous hill resorts were Naini Tal, Simla and Mussorie in north-west

India. Many attractive English villas are to be found all over these hill stations, and some of the best schools in India, schools for privileged families, are still to be found in these hill towns.

For a small village town like Kalimpong, other nationals had also made Kalimpong their home. Rich Tibetans owned property in Kalimpong and Darjeeling to take advantage of the missionary schools where they sent their children to learn English.

There were several Chinese families living in Kalimpong around the same period, with even a Chinese school of their own. They came under suspicion of the Indian government during the 1962 war with China, and some were forced to leave Kalimpong due to the sensitivity of the area. In later years, a number of Chinese immigrated to Hong Kong, others to China, some settled down in Calcutta and only a few remained in Kalimpong.

Darjeeling known as the Queen of the Hill Stations was then already famous for its tea plantations. When the British left, most of the plantations in Darjeeling and surrounding areas were left under the hands of the Anglo Indians.

In sharp contrast to Kalimpong, Darjeeling was a worldly, cosmopolitan town, and a popular tourist destination. Darjeeling had sophisticated shops, better hotels, and superior restaurants. If the people in Kalimpong needed a little excitement, they went to Darjeeling for the day.

Missionary schools in Darjeeling were older, larger and more expensive than in Kalimpong. The schools had children from countries as far away as Burma, Thailand, Pakistan and Malaysia. Unlike Kalimpong which enjoyed sunshine everyday of the year, the school children of Darjeeling looked forward to their unexpected sunshine holiday.

Darjeeling was then also famous for its two feet gauge railway line with its steam locomotive, lovingly called the Darjeeling Toy Train. The train pulled by a steam locomotive which for many years puffed and pulled and winded up the steep hills is still fully operational and retains its original features.

The Darjeeling Himalayan Railway (DHR) which is its official name, stretches 74 km. from Siliguri to Darjeeling. It made its maiden trip in September 1881, running through Tindhari, Kurseong, Sonada, then to Ghoom which at 2225 m. is among one of the highest known railway stations in the world, before arriving at its final destination in Darjeeling two kilometers away.

In 1999 the Darjeeling Himalayan Railway was given the World Heritage Status by UNESCO, so the Indian Government is now under the obligation of caring for the railway, and presenting a regular update to the UNESCO every five years. The DHR is only the second railway to have received this distinction, the first being the Semmering Railway in Austria.

The most plausible reason why Kalimpong was established as the base for Newar merchants travelling to Lhasa was the year round mild temperate climate, suitable to the Newars of Kathmandu. Darjeeling in comparison was cold and wet all the year round.

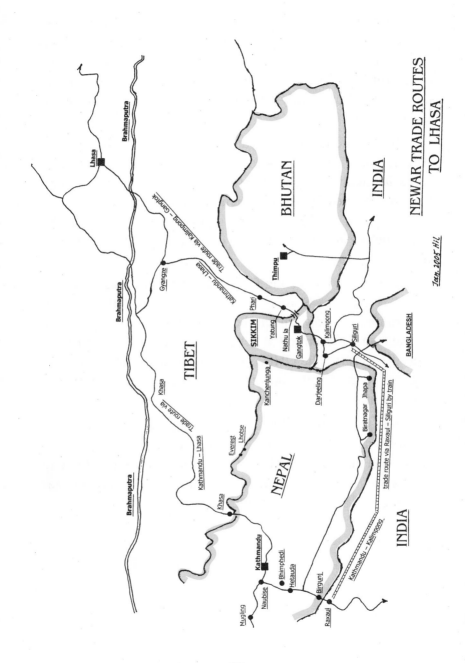

NEWAR TRADE ROUTES TO LHASA

Jan. 2005 Hit

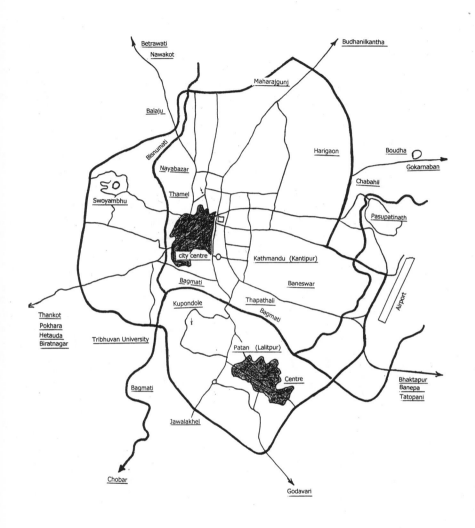

Betrawati
Nawakot

Budhanilkantha

Maharajgunj

Balaju

Bisnumati

Harigaon

Boudha
Gokarnaban

Nayabazar

Chabahil

Swoyambhu

Thamel

Pasupatinath

city centre

Kathmandu (Kantipur)

Bagmati

Baneswar

Kupondole

Thapathali

Airport

Bagmati

Thankot
Pokhara
Hetauda
Biratnagar

Tribhuvan University

Patan (Lalitpur)

Bhaktapur
Banepa
Tatopani

Bagmati

Centre

Jawalakhel

Chobar

Godavari

Kathmandu
Patan Jan. 2005
HiL
1300m

23

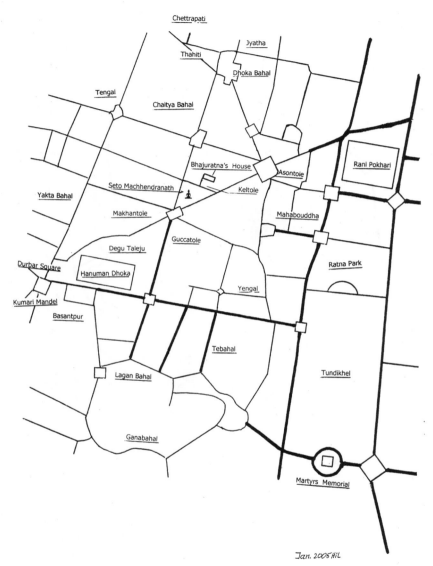

Jan. 2005 HiL

KATHMANDU CITY
CENTRE

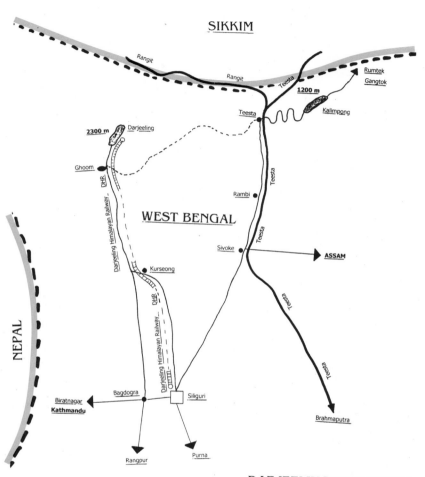

SIKKIM

Rangit

Rangit

Rumtek

Gangtok

Teesta

1200 m

Teesta

Kalimpong

2300 m

Darjeeling

Ghoom

DHR

Rambi

Teesta

WEST BENGAL

Teesta

Sivoke

ASSAM

Darjeeling Himalayan Railway

Kurseong

DHR

Teesta

NEPAL

Darjeeling Himalayan Railway

Biratnagar

Kathmandu

Bagdogra

Siliguri

Teesta

Rangpur

Purna

Brahmaputra

DARJEELING KALIMPONG
AREA   Jan 2005 Hil
(NOT TO SCALE)

25

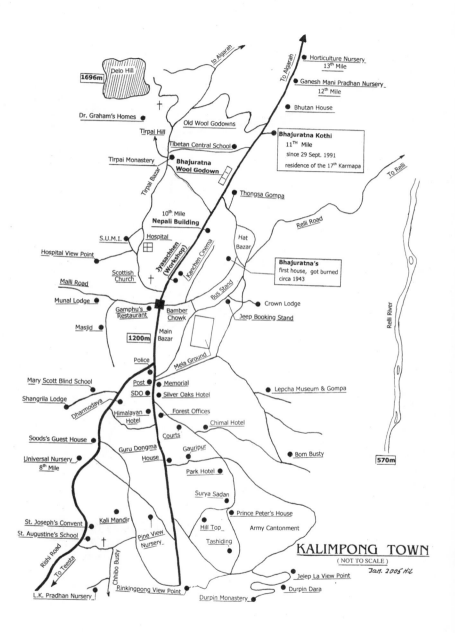

KALIMPONG TOWN
(NOT TO SCALE)
Jan. 2005 HL

Part One

Bhajuratna's Early Years

Bhajuratna was born at Kel Tole, in Kathmandu. According to the Newar lunar calendar the year was Nepal Sambat 1003 in the month of Poyela. According to the Nepali calendar it was Poush, the ninth month of Bikram Sambat 1940. Both dates roughly fall in December 1882. In Nepal, two different calendars are officially in use, the Bikram Sambat and the Gregorian while the third calendar Nepal Sambat is used only by the Newar community. Bikram Sambat (B.S.) starts from 58 B.C. is the current official era of Nepal, and Nepal Sambat (N.S.) which begins October of A.D. 879 marks the begin of the Newar New Year.

Kel Tole in the heart of Kathmandu, the ancient city of temples, is located beside the Janbahal temple complex. This is the temple of the goddess of *Seto Machendranath* – the White Avaloketeswar, the goddess of mercy. This is also the family temple of the Kansakars or Kasas as they are popularly referred to among the Newars. Bhajuratna's father Kulbir Singh Kansakar was according to family tradition a metal smith. It was a trade which remained within the Kansakar families and was passed on from father to son, as had been done for generations. The Kansakars produced the *kaan demas* – high rimmed heavy semi-bronze plates – used for the

27

daily mid-day and evening rice meals of the Newars. With daily use, this traditional household ware gleamed as though freshly polished.

Today with the common use of porcelain and with the introduction of cheap steel dinner bowls and plates these *kaan demas* have become a rarity, are too expensive and are used only for special family feasts.

Bhajuratna was the third of four sons born to Kulbir Singh Kansakar and his wife Nanibeti; the eldest and the youngest boys died as children. The family was not well off and had a difficult time trying to make ends meet as Kulbir Singh owned no workshop of his own. One night Bhajuratna overheard his parents talking worriedly about what to feed the children the next day. Anxious to help his parents, the next morning Bhajuratna went to a *kaka-baja* – grand uncle – who owned a metal workshop, to ask for work. By *bhaucha pueygu* – blowing flames with a bellow – Bhajuratna, then only four years old was given a few paisas daily which he proudly handed over to his mother.

During Newar festivals, it was the custom for the Kansakars to put up *kumba pyakhan* – a religious dance. Sons of rich families who wished to avoid taking part personally could in return for money hire somebody to dance for them. Bhajuratna therefore started taking up *kumba pyakhan* for rich families, and he continued earning money for the family in this manner for the next twelve years.

His father Kulbir Singh was one time imprisoned for not being able to pay off his debts. A bold and daring young boy Bhajuratna found a way to get his father out. One day he visited his father in the prison located at Ason Tole. Wrapped up in an oversized shawl, he managed to slip in unnoticed, and taking his father's place in the prison corner he forced his father to sneak out. Hours later, a prison warden discovering the little boy huddled in the corner, had him promptly thrown out.

As the parents were poor, Bhajuratna and his elder brother never had the opportunity to go to school. In 1898, when he was about sixteen years old he set off for Darjeeling with his elder brother Kulratna, to look for work. Like other fortune seekers before them, most of this long journey was done on foot, starting from Thankot to Kulekhani, then Bhimphedi and through other little villages to Birgunj, near the Indian border in the southern tip of Nepal. From Raxaul, on the Indian side of the border, the final leg of the journey to Siliguri, the junction for people travelling to Darjeeling, Kalimpong or Sikkim, was by train. These journeys to Darjeeling then took approximately five days.

Bhajuratna and his brother worked in Darjeeling for about five years for Muni Ratna Kansakar, a relative who owned a successful *bhusya* – metal workshop – by doing odd jobs and running on errands for him. When the brothers returned to Kathmandu with their savings in 1903 the parents made arrangements to get them married. Bhajuratna was married to Gyan Maya Tamrakar and Kulratna to Budhamaya. Arranged marriages where on the day of the wedding a young couple see each other for the first time in their life, were a tradition and quite normal for Newar families in those days, and is still an accepted practice even today.

Newar marriages are very expensive, elaborate, and the complicating ceremonial rites take at least four days to complete, and so to save expenses, most Newar families get all their sons of marriageable age married together on the same day. The extravagant Newar wedding put the family in debt so the same year after their marriage, Bhajuratna and his brother set off for Darjeeling again. This time to help clear their father's debt, leaving behind in Kathmandu their young wives.

Muni Ratna Kansakar of Darjeeling and Kul Muni Kansakar of Ghoom, a town two kilometers away from Darjeeling, gave them work again in their *bhusya* workshops. Kul Muni a handworker was another relative who had settled with his family in Ghoom. From these early years, Bhajuratna saw the importance of trade and realised that trade is one of the best and quickest means of earning money. Working in Darjeeling, he dreamt of setting up a shop in Kathmandu. With this in mind, he took the opportunity to travel to Bombay to buy textile for a future shop in Kathmandu. Leaving his brother Kulratna in Darjeeling, Bhajuratna returned to Kathmandu after two years, to set up a business with their combined savings.

Jog Bir Nayo, Bhajuratna's uncle, noticing that his nephew was an intelligent young boy helped him to set up a textile shop at Kel Tole, Bhajuratna's childhood neighbourhood. Within the following years, through his hard work, and with the help of his brother, Bhajuratna was able to extend his business to thirteen shops.

Young Bhajuratna was a tall slim moustached man, with a distinguished appearance. He was a man of authority, shrewd to his advantage but very honest, afraid of nobody, and in his early days loved a frequent drink. By nature he was choleric. He was in the habit of explicitly swearing when annoyed, a habit which accompanied him through all his later years. Though his sudden explosions fizzled out within seconds, he was feared by his subordinates, some dreaded him, but despite his short temper, he was respected by many he came into contact with. In comparison, his elder brother

Kulratna was completely different, and quietly depended on the outspoken, quick thinking Bhajuratna.

1918 was a tragic year for Bhajuratna, when fire broke out at Kel Tole. With help from all the neighbours, the fire was finally brought under control, but not before it had completely destroyed four of his shops. This was a severe loss to Bhajuratna and the family, as most of the expensive merchandise including property had gone up in flames. Repairs had to be done to the damaged property, and loans taken for setting up the shops could no longer be settled. Bhajuratna planned to go to Darjeeling again, but circumstances prevented him from leaving Kathmandu immediately.

Once more, and in the same year, fate again struck Bhajuratna an unkind blow. His wife Gyan Maya Tamrakar died due to a fever contracted while fasting during the holy Buddhist month of *gunla* – which falls after the dark moon in July – leaving behind four young children. Gyan Prabha born 1908, Laxmi Prabha born 1910, Laxmi Hera in 1913 and son Maniharsha Jyoti in 1917. Bhajuratna had to postpone his plan to go to Darjeeling, and circa 1919 he remarried. It was only after two years that he could finally leave for Darjeeling again to earn money, to make up for the losses incurred to his business. This time he left behind his second wife Gyan Maya Tuladhar with the four young children, and a four month old son Gyan Jyoti born 1921.

Bhajuratna once again headed straight for Muni Ratna Kansakar at Hari Das Hatta in Darjeeling. This brass and copper smith family was running a thriving business producing cymbals for Tibetan monasteries. He also went to Kul Muni Kansakar in Ghoom.

This time, conditions were different, Bhajuratna was a *sahu* a shopkeeper or businessman himself due to his cloth shops in Kathmandu. The two cousins were reluctant to give him work again as they felt that the work available with them was now below his status. They suggested he go to Kalimpong to set up his own business instead. This was a good opportunity for him to start, as all their goods were taken to Kalimpong to be sold to Tibetan merchants living there. From Kalimpong, almost all their ware were then sent on to Lhasa. Whatever Bhajuratna required was available with them, and all he had to do now was to look for a shop to rent in Kalimpong.

Settling Down in Kalimpong

Soon after arriving in Darjeeling, Bhajuratna taking the advise of his two cousins, left for Kalimpong. From Darjeeling he travelled on foot to Kalimpong with his faithful and loyal servant Thulecha, a *Tamang* – an ethnic Nepali – who was to serve Bhajuratna for many many years.

Enough ware had been bought in Darjeeling to resell in Kalimpong which Thulecha carried on his back in a *doko* – a large bamboo basket commonly used by Nepali porters for transporting goods. The *doko* has a broad band and the carrier carries the load on his back supporting the full weight of the load up to 50 kg. with his forehead, thus leaving both his hands free to support himself while ascending or descending the steep foot paths.

On arriving in Kalimpong, Bhajuratna stayed with Purna Bir and Harkha Bir Shakya of Patan Kathmandu, while he searched for a shop to rent. They were rich and firmly established Lhasa traders, well known to all the Newars in Kalimpong. Two days later, Bhajuratna rented his first shop which was located below 10th Mile, right in the centre of the town. In Kalimpong, Darjeeling and Gangtok, and in other towns in these areas, places have been commonly referred to in this manner and this practical system is very much in use even today.

Bhajuratna's rented shop which was also to serve him as his home, was on the way down the hill to what is still today known as Hath Bazar, where every Wednesday and Saturday the village market was held. This festive tradition is carried on in Kalimpong to the present day, and is a great attraction for the young and the old.

The shop which Bhajuratna had found belonged to Kodamal Jethmal, a *Marwari* family – Indians originally from Rajasthan who have established themselves all over India as a successful class of business people – and the shop together with an adjoining room was rented for the monthly sum of fifteen rupees. It was here that Bhajuratna began to sell his first bronze, brass and copper ware which he had brought from Darjeeling, all that his Tamang servant Thulecha could carry in his *doko*.

Starting a Workshop
in Kalimpong

As business prospered, Thulecha had to be sent to Darjeeling to bring more goods to restock the shop in Kalimpong. After a few months, these buying trips became more frequent, Bhajuratna seemed to be selling his ware faster than had been anticipated. Kul Muni of Ghoom finally said to Bhajuratna: "Why don't you bring your own handworkers from Kathmandu? This will save you the trouble of coming to Darjeeling everytime you needed ware to stock up your shop." He realised this was true so he took his cousin's advise. He had a letter sent to his older brother Kulratna Kansakar in Kathmandu, explained to him his intention of setting up a workshop in Kalimpong, and asked him to send to Kalimpong some Newar copper and brass smiths.

All arrangements confirmed, Kulratna travelled to Kalimpong circa 1922 accompanied by Bhajuratna's son Maniharsha Jyoti, his own son Ratna Jyoti, and four *kalighars* – hand workers – and among them was Tushin Rajkarnikar, Dharma Das's father. (Dharma Das and his brothers today live in Chettrapati, Kathmandu, with their families, and run a very popular and thriving Newari sweet shop).

Bhajuratna had never been to school, but had over the years taught himself to read and write. There was only one school in Kathmandu, the Durbar School for the Rana children and the very privileged. He now realized the importance of a good education, so he was glad to have the possibility of sending the two young boys to a school in Kalimpong, where he had a wide choice of schools. They were admitted to the Scottish Universities Mission Institute, popularly known to the locals as SUMI, which ran a school for boys, and was not far from where Bhajuratna lived.

Bhajuratna's workshop was set up at the 10th Mile. It was a long wooden building next to today's Kanchen Cinema Hall, and was simply called *jyasachhen* or workshop in Newari. The *jyasachhen* has changed very little even to this day. The highly demanded copper, brass and bronze ware, specialised items for household use, were now produced by Bhajuratna's own *kalighars*, and business continued to thrive. Among the various hand produced household ware were *pusabata* – sets of large open brass bowls, *khasi* – copper cauldrons – and *momo bharas* – three to four tier brass and copper vessels for steaming dumplings.

Due to increasing demands, and an expanding business, additional hand workers were required for Kalimpong. It was not until four years later, that another batch of Newar *kalighars* from Kathmandu travelled to Kalimpong as required by Bhajuratna. They were accompanied by his wife Gyan Maya, and his now four year old son Gyan Jyoti. Also accompanying them was Tushin's wife.

For Tushin's wife, it was no simple matter trying to leave Kathmandu to join her husband in Kalimpong. In Newar families, life was not easy for a daughter-in-law. She had no say in household affairs, and needed to get permission from her husband's parents for every action she wished to undertake. Even for a day off to visit her parents. A daughter-in-law had to subdue her feelings and thoughts and had to often change her own plans for the whims of her mother-in-law.

It was therefore against the wishes of her in-laws that Tushin's wife took the bold initiative of going to Kalimpong. The common means of transport then was a *doolie* – palanquin, a covered or uncovered framework carried by three to four men. Hidden inside a *doolie* and with the help of Bhajuratna's wife she managed to escape unnoticed to Thankot, from where the same day they set off for Bhimphedi.

Another common method of transport was in a *tamdan* – a litter chair – which was slung on a pole and carried by two men.

Bhajuratna was happy to have his wife in Kalimpong, and his small son whom he had last seen as a four month old baby. Gyan Jyoti was immediately admitted to the Kindergarten section of the Girls High School, also run by the Scottish Missionary, and just a walking distance from home. As he grew older, he was transferred to the SUMI boys school.

Syamukapu – the Beginning

Tushin died of cholera while still working in Kalimpong, leaving behind a helpless young wife with three small sons. Bhajuratna anxious to do something for her asked her how he could be helpful. She informed him about her background as the daughter of a sweet maker of Patan, Kathmandu, and about her childhood and early teenage years which had been spent helping her parents prepare sweets for the family sweet shop. Bhajuratna had a solution, he suggested that she do the thing she was good at, she was to start making sweets for a living.

With the help of Bhajuratna's wife Gyan Maya, the two women set about making *chiriboka* at the back of Bhajuratna's tiny rented shop, the shop located on the way to Hath Bazar. This *chiriboka* was made of plain granulated sugar, melted slightly and quickly formed into little balls.

This sweet known as *yelachingra* in Kathmandu was in those days also very popular among the Newars of Kathmandu. There were no sweets those days, so in Kalimpong *chiriboka* began to sell like hot-cakes among the Tibetans and Nepalis and the other locals of the town. They became so popular that Tibetans coming to Kalimpong started buying the *chiribokas* in sacks, with each sack weighing approximately forty kilos. Between five to ten sacks were regularly sold to the *thebas* – Tibetan load carriers – who were returning to Tibet empty with their train of mules.

Every *theba*, every Tibetan trader on coming to Kalimpong, did not leave without first buying *chiribokas*. They were all drawn to this sweet like bees to honey. They searched, they asked and were directed to Bhajuratna's tiny shop. All were directed to the little shop near the two large trees on the way down to Hath Bazar. If they were still unable to find Bhajuratna's little shop, they were given a description of the man who owned the shop, the man wearing a white cap, *Syamukapu* in Tibetan.

As weeks and months went by, Bhajuratna was being referred to as *Syamukapu* by not only the Tibetans, but also the Nepalis, the Newars, the Marwaris, and the other locals of Kalimpong when giving direction to Tibetans who wanted to buy the *chiribokas*, as *chiribokas* were available only with *Syamukapu*. The high popularity of *chiriboka,* was an additional boost to Bhajuratna's family undertaking.

A Deal with the Thebas

All these years, the transport of merchandise with mule
caravans for all Newar merchants or Lhasa Sahus as they
were commonly referred to, was undertaken by Purna Bir
Harkha Bir (two Shakya brothers who ran business under this
name in Kalimpong). One day, Triratna Man Tuladhar who
was on a visit to Kalimpong happened to be at Bhajuratna's
shop paying him a courtesy visit. He spent almost the whole
day observing the *thebas* buying sack loads of *chiribokas* to
take back to Tibet. He waited patiently until all was quiet
again in the shop and then said, "*Paju*, – uncle – why don't
you take up the task of sending goods to Tibet yourself,
instead of sending them through the Newar middlemen? The
thebas have to go back to Tibet anyway with their unladen
mules, and with so many *thebas* coming to you, you have with
all their mules put together enough animals to carry your
loads for you to Tibet"

Bhajuratna always open to suggestions, thought over it
and finally tried out this new idea. At the next opportunity he
asked one of the *thebas* to take his ware for him to Phari – a
Tibetan village half way to Lhasa – at a twenty-five paisa
cheaper rate than the normal fare, as he had to go back to
Tibet anyway and he was going back without any load. After
a bit of persuasion, and a little threat not to sell him *chiribokas*
Bhajuratna got his way as the *theba* was unwilling to leave
without his *chiribokas*. Gradually he also got the other *thebas*

to agree to take his loads for him to Phari, and at the bargained price.

The *thebas* were a hardy, tough race of Tibetans, honest and very reliable, used to the inclement Tibetan weather, familiar with their way around the treacherous routes and narrow passes leading to Tibet and onward to Lhasa. Bhajuratna had made a good bargain, he knew his goods were in safe dependable hands and that they would be delivered safely to Phari.

As weeks went by, the Lhasa Sahus heard that Bhajuratna was having his goods taken to Phari by the *thebas* at a rate cheaper than what they were paying for. They came and requested Bhajuratna that he ask the *thebas* to take their ware to Phari too, as the *thebas* would only listen to him.

Slowly, in the following months, Bhajuratna was undertaking responsibility for the transport of goods to Tibet for many of the Newar merchants too.

An Influential Man
in Kalimpong

Bhajuratna's trade prospered and with it his popularity and his influence. As his popularity grew his shop started becoming the meeting point in the evenings for the Newar merchants, the Tibetans and the Marwaris. Bhajuratna's shop became the place to discuss business, the place for obtaining new information, and the place for all matters concerning the latest on trade to Tibet.

Often a Marwari merchant would inform Bhajuratna that a certain Tibetan was in Kalimpong looking for a special merchandise, would Bhajuratna be kind enough to put in a word to this Tibetan regarding the goods available with him. Bhajuratna made it clear that he wanted nothing to do with any commission for himself for these business deals, but he agreed to bring the prospective business partners into contact, if the Marwari merchant was willing to sell his ware to the Tibetan at a slightly lower rate than that of the market price. This agreed, Bhajuratna brought the two traders into contact, and a deal would be settled.

News spread. The Newar merchants learning that a certain *Marwari* was selling a particular ware at a lower rate to some Tibetan, without further delay bought their goods too directly from the same Marwari. Later on comparing prices they discovered that the price offered to Bhajuratna was always lower than the price offered to them directly by the Marwari himself.

The traders realised that it was more profitable to get Bhajuratna to make the deal for them with the Marwari, or to let him buy the merchandise on their behalf, than to do it directly themselves.

As weeks went by, more traders sought help from Bhajuratna, and he soon found himself becoming the most sought after and influential middleman in Kalimpong.

Bhajuratna/Syamukapu Kothi in Phari

Insurance of merchandise seemed to be unknown in this part of the world during those early prosperous trading years. Loss of goods due to robberies or accidents on treacherous rivers and along dangerous narrow trails were common. The route to Phari was dangerous, and no trader could be sure if his goods would arrive safely at Phari, or even Lhasa.

At Phari, the Himalayan foothills ended, and the Tibetan plateau began. A cold barren place Phari was frozen all the year round, and according to the Lhasa Newars, if a Newar survived it to Phari, then he would manage the rest of the way to Lhasa too.

In 1930 Bhajuratna established his *kothi* – house – a shop cum residential building in Phari. Asa Ratna Tamrakar, his first wife's brother and *Paju* – maternal uncle to Maniharsha, was sent to Phari as its first *thakali* – chief or head of business.

The establishment of a Bhajuratna *kothi* at Phari was definitely good news to the Newar Traders who were sending goods to Lhasa through Bhajuratna. Now with Phari as a half way station between Lhasa and Gangtok, letters sent from Phari with a post runner or post rider regarding arrival or loss of goods could reach their relatives or representatives in Lhasa within four to five days.

The Lhasa Newars were confident that goods entrusted to Bhajuratna were safe under his charge. They had full faith in his choice of *thebas*. Till now, Newar traders had very often to accept without question stories about loss of goods through accidents or attacks from wayside bandits, and there was no way of proving whether they were being cheated or not, as was the practise carried out by some of the muleteers. Fortunately, they were the few exceptions.

The Earthquake of 1934

One day, on a beautiful sunny winter afternoon in Kathmandu, most people were out enjoying the sunshine, as they did everyday. They were on rooftops, on their terraces, in the sunny courtyards, or sitting on the steps of temples. Others were sitting outside their tiny shops, in a sunny corner, as they waited for customers.

Suddenly the dogs started howling, and birds took flight in panic. They were instinctively reacting to an impending danger. People shouted back at the howling dogs to keep shut, as to the superstitious Nepalis it meant a prediction of approaching evil.

Unexpectedly the ground started swaying, and buildings started collapsing. People were screaming and shouting: "Earthquake! Earthquake!" and all scrambled to get out of their houses as fast as they could.

It was January 1934 (1990 B.S), two o'clock in the afternoon, when the earthquake struck Nepal. It measured 8.4 in the Richter scale. The epicentre was along the Nepal Bihar border. Kathmandu was effected severely by this earthquake resulting in heavy damages in the valley. It left 17,871 people dead, 3,379 wounded, more than 200,000 houses, temples and historical buildings destroyed.

Family members were separated in the ensuing confusion. This was one of the worst earthquakes that anybody could ever remember. Kathmandu resembled the aftermath of a battle, like a city damaged by an air-raid. About the same time, people living in Kalimpong also felt the waves of the earthquake, it was severe enough to topple the steeple of the Scottish Missionary Church.

In Kathmandu itself, very few were unaware of what was actually happening. Like several other Newars, two young women were walking to the Swoyambhu temple, as they did every day, when they felt the earthquake. From the slopes of the Swoyambhu hill they turned back for a view of the Kathmandu valley, and were surprised to see a cloud of dust covering the city. It was only later as they headed for home at the end of their walk around the Swoyambhu hill, in those years surrounded only by fields, that they realised something was terribly wrong.

They came across damaged houses, saw people running around crying, shouting, running to each other for help. The two women, walking back from Swoyambhu finally panicked and ran all the way in the direction to their homes. They had to scramble over crumbled walls and bricks strewn over the narrow streets, to search for their children and family members. The younger woman to search for her two year old daughter, Laxmi Prabha, who in later years would be Gyan Jyoti's future wife.

It is interesting to note that many people in Nepal, particularly the older generation, use the year of the great earthquake as a reference date to remember their age. When asked their age, the answers may be, "I was a six year old when the earthquake happened." "I was born five years after the *nabaysal* – year ninety – earthquake." Or, "I had started wearing a sari when the earthquake took place." Meaning the woman was roughly twelve or thirteen years old at the time of the quake.

Tundikhel, the large open parade ground in the middle of Kathmandu was a commotion of people, as all had gathered there to get away from the collapsing houses in the narrow streets and alleys. Some found their missing relatives and children there in the chaos, but many were not so fortunate.

The young woman returning from Swoyambhu finally found her wailing two year old daughter at Tundikhel. In the ensuing confusion and panic, a man from the neighbourhood had picked up the two year old with two other small children in his arms had rushed with them to the safety of the parade ground. Many continued living in the open even after a few weeks. Some because they had no home to go back to, and others because they were afraid of being buried in their houses in the recurring tremors.

There were tales from people losing a friend, a child or relative as they sat chatting together, saved from death by the fraction of an inch. There were endless tales of sorrow and of wonder, that circled around Kathmandu for days, as people started rebuilding their damaged houses and began to pick up their shattered lives.

Maniharsha Jyoti

Bhajuratna's elder son Maniharsha, born 1917, arrived in Kalimpong with his *taba* Kulratna and cousin Ratna Jyoti, with the first batch of *kalighars* in 1922. He was admitted to the Kalimpong Scottish Missionary School with his cousin. In 1927 Maniharsha was sent to Calcutta to continue his schooling and to live with Dhamman Sahu, a rich and well established Lhasa Newar, whose firm was called Dharma Man Purna Man. They had an office cum apartment at Harrison Road, which was Maniharsha's home for the next few years.

The mutual agreement was that Bhajuratna would take no commission for goods sent on their behalf to Tibet, and in exchange Maniharsha was to receive free board and lodging with them to enable him to go to school. In return for all this arrangement, the young boy would work for them according to his capacity whenever he was home from school. The month long school summer holidays were often spent with his own parents in Kalimpong. In this hard watchful manner Maniharsha spent his young teenage years in Calcutta until 1933, when at the age of sixteen, he passed his Matriculation (class 10) from Calcutta and returned to Kalimpong.

In the same year following his return from Calcutta after successfully completing his schooling, Bhajuratna thought it fit to get his elder son involved with the business world. He discussed his thoughts with his wife Gyan Maya, and they came to the decision that the best solution would be to let him start in Kathmandu, where he himself had gained his first experience.

Maniharsha was sent to Kathmandu with five thousand Nepali rupees to help him set up a shop. The young son was accompanied to Kathmandu by Dev Ratna Kansakar, his *taba* – paternal elder uncle – and Bhajuratna's first cousin.

As soon as news reached Kalimpong about the earthquake in Nepal, and about the serious damages and high death toll in Kathmandu, Bhajuratna immediately left for Kathmandu. He had to find out if his elder son Maniharsha was safe, and also to check on damages to his house. Miraculously nothing happened to his son nor to the old family house at Kel Tole, but the neighbouring houses sustained severe damages.

It was shortly after the earthquake that Bhajuratna's uncle Jogbir Aba passed away. Bhajuratna then bought his uncle's house which adjoined his own. Once the new ownership changed hands, he had the house completely renovated. Many months later, he also bought Bhote Baja's house, which was connected to the other end of his own house and had it renovated too.

Maniharsha was left in Kathmandu when Bhajuratna returned to Kalimpong after two weeks. Unfortunately business did not prosper as expected for the young boy in Kathmandu. He sent a message to his father asking for additional money to help him out of his climbing debts, instead Bhajuratna had his son immediately recalled to Kalimpong in 1935.

It was around this period that Pasang Tempa happened to be at Bhajuratna's shop in Kalimpong. Pasang Tempa worked as Chief Accountant for Panda Tshang, a rich and influential Tibetan, who was then the Governor of Dhomo. Dhomo, or Yatung as it was more popularly known to non-Tibetans, was the location of the Tibetan government's minting house.

While waiting in the shop, Pasang Tempa watched Bhajuratna weighing and selling *chapu* – scraps of copper and brass – to the other traders. He was curious and wanted to know what they did with all the *chapu,* and was naturally very surprised to learn that the scraps could be smelted and resold as new metal. Scrap metal from Kalimpong was sent to middle-men in Calcutta in big bundles, and the brass and copper sheets required for Bhajuratna's workshop came from Calcutta.

Through Pasang Tempa Bhajuratna came to hear of the Tibetan mint at Yatung, where scrap copper was lying around the yard in heaps, discarded as waste, as no one knew what to do with them. Would Syamukapu be interested in buying *chapu* lying around Dhomo? Bhajuratna was of course interested, and certainly had no problem sending somebody to buy all the *chapu* lying around Dhomo/Yatung.

Maniharsha was chosen to go to Yatung in 1935 to buy scrap copper. Fifty to sixty loads of *chapu* were collected and bought from the Tibetan mint, each load weighing forty kilos. While in Yatung, Maniharsha took the opportunity to visit the Bhajuratna Syamukapu *kothi* at Phari, he made a tour of the place and then travelled back to Yatung before returning to Kalimpong. In all he was away from Kalimpong for a week. The next time he set foot in Tibet would be more than thirty years later.

In 1944, a double wedding took place. It was an arranged marriage, where the brides were selected by Bhajuratna and his wife Gyan Maya. On the same day that Maniharsha Jyoti was married to Keshari Laxmi, his cousin Ratna Jyoti was married to Dan Laxmi.

Bhajuratna Kothi in Calcutta

A good deal of merchandise required by the Lhasa Newars flowed between Calcutta and Kalimpong. Much of this trade was organised through the handful of Newar businessmen who had offices in Calcutta. Many of the Lhasa Newars were by now doing their business through Bhajuratna in Kalimpong and Phari, who had through the years earned himself the trust of all business men due to his honesty, openness and reliability.

Bhajuratna was often approached by the Lhasa Newars to buy their goods for them from Calcutta, "If you have a *kothi* in Calcutta, you could take over this responsibility on behalf of all the Lhasa Newars of Kalimpong," was their suggestion. Bhajuratna already in a good financial position to do what was requested of him, and always wanting to help his fellow men, seriously set about looking for a base in Calcutta.

An agreement was made with the reputed Lhasa Newar Buddha Ratna Bodhi Ratna Tuladhar (in later years father-in-law to Bhajuratna's youngest son Dev Jyoti). They were old established traders known as Moti Chong Kong to the Tibetans. Bhajuratna was allowed to share their Calcutta premises to carry out his business, and was also permitted to equally share in the monthly rent.

Maha Ratna Shakya, Bhajuratna's *twae* or *meet* brother – a ceremonial brother or sister relationship common among

Newars to a non-related person – was chosen to be sent to Calcutta.

Being a *twae* is a life long relationship for both partners, with each being honoured as a family member and invited to participate in the other family's celebrations such as annual feasts, religious festivals, marriages and death ceremonies.

In 1937 Maha Ratna Shakya travelled to Calcutta as Bhajuratna's *thakali* – chief – and with him went Maniharsha. And so, Bhajuratna's first Calcutta business was set up, operating from the already existing establishment of Buddha Ratna Bodhi Ratna, at 40A Armenian Street.

Syamukapu Kothi in Lhasa

Bhajuratna's cousin brother Heraratna Kansakar, his *taba's* son – son of his father's elder brother, was employed as *thakali* of Chik Kazi Raja Bhai company in Lhasa. After living there nearly nine years continuously, he left Lhasa in 1938. From his many years in the Tibetan capital, Heraratna was already an experienced business man and knew everything about running a Lhasa *kothi*. While Heraratna was still in Kalimpong preparing to return to his family in Kathmandu, Bhajuratna confided to him his desire to open his own *kothi* in Lhasa, and asked the Lhasa veteran if he could help him to set up the new shop.

Heraratna agreed to do this favour for his cousin, on condition that after two years somebody would relieve him from his post, as he was now not willing to spend more than two years in Lhasa. A gentleman's agreement was made. Heraratna first visited his family in Kathmandu and after a year returned to Kalimpong.

Shortly after his return, Heraratna left for Lhasa in 1939 to set up Bhajuratna's Lhasa *kothi*. With himself as *thakali* – chief or head – he was accompanied by his younger brother Sanuratna, and Hari Lal of Ghoom, who was Bhajuratna's *banja* – assistant worker – in Kalimpong.

Bhajuratna's business flourished with each passing month and year. With Hera Ratna working for him in Lhasa, with *kalighars* in Kalimpong producing his ware for Lhasa, a *kothi* in Calcutta, a *kothi* in Phari, dozens of *banjas* employed by him, and sons Maniharsha Jyoti and Gyan Jyoti to help him, he was a contended prosperous man.

With several other well to do merchants like Bhajuratna permanently residing in Kalimpong, the little town was the hub of trade and activity. Goods were endlessly arriving or leaving Kalimpong. There was the constant movement of pack mules and donkeys, and with the bells worn by the animals endlessly jingling and jangling with every movement, they grew to be the familiar sights and sounds of Kalimpong.

Heraratna sent his cousin a letter in early 1942 reminding him that his two years in Lhasa were already up and that somebody was to be sent to replace him as *thakali*. Bhajuratna's first reaction was to ask his elder son Maniharsha to go to Lhasa to relieve Heraratna. He refused. Maniharsha had lived several years in Calcutta while doing his schooling, had seen Yatung and Phari when he had gone there to buy scrap copper for his father, and knew what Tibet had to offer. He was reluctant to return to the wilderness of Tibet and preferred to go to the *kothi* in Calcutta instead.

Bhajuratna's next option was to ask his second son Gyan Jyoti to go to Lhasa. He also refused as he had already registered himself for college and wanted to continue his studies. Bhajuratna and his wife were worried that they would be unable to fulfil their promise to Heraratna. Despite his worry, he was unwilling to send somebody he did not know well, as his *thakali* for Lhasa. His wife who shared his burden could not keep back her tears. One day Gyan Jyoti saw his mother in tears and learned from her about the promise his father had made to Heraratna. As the sons were unwilling to go to Lhasa, she was afraid that the old father would now have to undertake the difficult and long journey himself. Gyan

Jyoti now changed his mind and agreed to go to Lhasa as *thakali* to take over responsibility from Heraratna, the older Newar.

The auspicious day for Gyan Jyoti's departure for Lhasa was fixed. It was to be 6th December 1942. A *Bhinapuja* – an elaborate religious ceremony to pray for a traveller's safe journey – was performed for Gyan Jyoti's forthcoming and first journey to Tibet.

These Lhasa years were memorable years for Gyan Jyoti, a pet subject when narrating travel tales to his children and grandchildren in later years. After the rich green landscape of Kalimpong, with its blossoming trees and hedges, wild flowers in every nook and cranny, the Tibetan landscape was a stark contrast. The barrenness of the arid Tibetan plateau was at first strange and in its strangeness fascinating, but with each passing day, it made him very depressed, and sometimes the depressing feeling even made him want to cry. Once the sight of just a single leaf on a naked tree was enough to lift his spirit and cheered him up for the rest of the day.

In 1944 Gyan Jyoti returned from his first trip to Tibet, after completing two successful years there, bringing back with him money and fame for his father and the family. He was replaced by Ratna Jyoti as *thakali* for the next two and a half years.

Expulsion of Buddhist Monks from Nepal

In 1926, Chandra Sumsher, the Rana ruler of this period (1901–1929) expelled five Nepali Mahayana monks – Mahapragya, Mahachhyanti, Mahachandra, Mahabirje and Mahagyan – together with their Tibetan Guru Rinpoche Tshering Norbhu, from Nepal, for preaching and spreading Buddhism in the country. Rinpoche Tshering Norbhu had also ordained them as Mahayana monks, making them the pioneer Nepali Mahayana monks in Nepal.

The banished monks intended to travel to Lhasa, and on their way made a stop at Kalimpong where they were warmly welcomed and assisted by the Newar traders residing there. Bhajuratna personally provided them with *bhojan-daan* – donation of food – and lodging during their entire sojourn in Kalimpong. The monks were so well looked after, that their original intention of staying for only a few days was extended to eight months, after which they journeyed on to Tibet.

Around the same time, Shree Dharmaditya Dharmacharya, a famous Nepali Theravada Buddhist scholar was living in Kalimpong, He was the first to lay the foundation of Theravada Buddhism in Kalimpong, by establishing a Nepali Buddhist Library at a small rented house, in 1927. He propagated Buddhism to the local residents, and was also the first to celebrate Buddha Jayanti in Kalimpong with great pomp and splendour, which from then on became established as a festive annual event in this little hill town.

Mahapragya (1901–1979) who had gone to Tibet as a Mahayana monk with the other four exiled monks and their Guru Rinpoche Tshering Norbhu, returned to Kalimpong after a couple of years, but influenced by the teachings of Shree Dharmaditya Dharmacharya, he converted to Theravada Buddhism. From Tibet, Karmashil Gheshe of Nepal arrived in Kalimpong in 1930 as a Tibetan Mahayana monk, and also influenced by Shree Dharmaditya Dharmacharya and Mahapragya Bhikkhu he became interested in Theravada Buddhism. He undertook a pilgrimage to the Buddhist holy places around India with Mahapragya Bhikkhu, and became Sramaner Pragyananda at Kushinagar. Later Pragyananda journeyed on to Burma to further study Theravada Buddhism, and was there ordained a Theravada Bhikkhu.

In the Buddhist countries of Burma, Thailand and Sri Lanka, education was free for Theravada monks and nuns, and it is still the practice today. This was therefore the reason behind the Buddhists of Nepal travelling to one of these countries if they wished to join the Theravada order. Theravada monks after ordination are called Bhikkhus. Non-ordained monks are referred to as *Sramaner*, and nuns are *Anagarika*.

Around 1936 Bhajuratna bought a small house together with a little plot of land at Tirpai hill, an area which is located uphill between the 10th and 11th Mile, and above the Tibetan School. This was later referred to as the Pragya Chaitya Mahavihar, and was installed with a Buddha statue personally chiselled and polished by Mahapragya himself.

Amritananda of Kathmandu (in later years a renowned Theravada Bhikkhu) became a *Sramaner* of the Theravada order at Kushinagar and came to Kalimpong in 1936 to study under the guidance of Mahapragya Bhikkhu who was still living in Kalimpong.

Some months later, Sramaner Amritananda went to Bhojpur in Eastern Nepal, and three weeks later Mahapragya Bhikkhu followed him, to propagate Buddhism in Nepal, assuming that the ban on preaching Buddhism in Nepal had been lifted.

Unfortunately this was not so. The Rana government hearing of Mahapragya's return to Nepal despite his exile, had both Mahapragya Bhikkhu and Sramaner Amritananda imprisoned at the Bhojpur jail. From Bhojpur, they were both deported to the Dhankuta jail and finally to Jogbani the Indian border post in eastern Nepal.

Days later, bound hand and foot, both monks were brought to Kalimpong by the police. They went directly to Bhajuratna with their prisoners, "Are these your men?" they asked. Astounded, he replied "Yes."

Only then were the two monks relieved of their bounds and handed over to Bhajuratna.

Some weeks later, with financial help from the Newars of Kalimpong, Sramaner Amritananda journeyed on to Burma. From there he later travelled to Sri Lanka to study Buddhism, and in Sri Lanka he was some years later ordained a Theravada Bhikkhu.

Another dark year for the Buddhists of Nepal was 1944. This time all the Theravada monks living in Kathmandu were expelled from Nepal by Juddha Sumsher, the Rana ruler (1932–1945). They were Bhikkhus Pragyananda, Dharmalok, Subhodanandal and Pragyarashim. The Sramaners included Pragyaras, Ratnajyoti, Agadhamma and Kumar Kashyap.

Bhajuratna came to hear about this, and was once more ready to help the monks.

Before the monks left Kathmandu, Bhajuratna sent his elder daughter Gyan Shova to Thankot with money which she was to hand over to the monks. As the monks slowly walked past the village post of Thankot, the start of their journey to India, Gyan Shova handed over to each of the exiled monks an envelope containing money from her father. They were all instructed to travel to Kalimpong, if they were ever in need of help.

Most went into exile to Saranath India, while a few chose to travel to Kalimpong.

Buddhist Centre
in Kalimpong

The Theravada monks who had decided to travel to Kalimpong were warmly welcomed by the Newar residents of Kalimpong, and Bhajuratna once more happily provided them with *bhojan daan* – food donation – and lodging and all the necessary expenses for as long as they wished to remain in Kalimpong. The other monks who had gone to Saranath were unable to remain there for an indefinite period, due to the hot climate and for financial reasons. Hearing of the generous *bhojan-daan* and facilities provided by Bhajuratna Kansakar, they also travelled to Kalimpong.

It was from Kalimpong that the Bhikkhus and Sramaners were able to decide about their future. With financial support from the Newars of Kalimpong they had the means of travelling to Burma or Sri Lanka, to continue their studies in Buddhism.

By now, many Theravada monks were residing in Kalimpong, with different Newar families, and some at Bhajuratna's house. To ease this situation, the Newar traders decided to buy a house so the monks could live and pray together under one roof.

The Newar and Tibetan traders started collecting donations with this intention, but with everybody contributing between one and ten rupees, some fifty rupees, and a rare hundred rupees, the amount collected was far below what was required. Bhajuratna then contributed the failing amount of sixteen thousand rupees and a building called Elza Villa at the 9th Mile was bought in 1947. This was renamed Dharmodaya Vihar.

The choice of buying Elza Villa was much criticised by some of the Newars of Kalimpong, as to them it did not seem appropriate to convert the house of an Englishman into a Buddhist place of worship.

In the next few years, a *chaitya* – a stupa – was also built within its compound where both monks and Buddhist followers could gather together and pray. The foundation stone for constructing the stupa was laid by Ananda Kaushalyan Bhikkhu, while Vivekananda Bhikkhu and Gyan Sagar Bhikkhu personally undertook to level out the site where the stupa now stands, and Mahapant Bhikkhu designed and tended the garden around the Dharmodaya Vihar.

When the shrine was completed, a beautiful marble Buddha presented by the Burmese Buddhists was installed there. A cemented path around the Vihar was also added in the following months, and a few months later, a gate in the style of Sanchi was constructed.

Circa 1948, the distinguished Narad Bhikkhu of Sri Lanka arrived in Kalimpong to participate in a crucial meeting. The monks and Newar traders met to discuss the means of approaching the Rana government of Nepal, to revoke their existing exile law against the Buddhist monks, to enable the Newar monks to return to their home country.

A five member delegation under Narad Bhikkhu together with Bhikkhu Amritnananda approached the Rana Prime Minister Padma Sumsher (1945–1948) in Kathmandu, and they finally came to a successful agreement. The exile law was abrogated and the Buddhist monks were once more permitted to return to Nepal.

Circa 1949 land within the courtyard of Shreegha Vihar, near Thahity in Kathmandu, was bought by Bhajuratna. A double storied house was built and then donated to the Theravada monks. The monks returning to Kathmandu now had a place to reside in, beside the already existing Anandakuthi Vihar below Swoyambhunath.

Kalimpong meanwhile had grown to become a centre for Buddhism and was often visited by Buddhist scholars and monks and other distinguished visitors. They came to Kalimpong specially during the hot summer months when most of India was under a hot spell. But summer or winter, Kalimpong has a mild temperate climate all the year round.

The Newar community of Kalimpong grew to be proud of their Dharmodaya Vihar.

Special Honours

Bhajuratna's help to the Buddhist community did not go unnoticed by the Rana government of Nepal. He was one day summoned to Darjeeling. He had no idea why, and his family members were afraid for him, fearing he would be arrested for helping the banished Buddhist monks.

To their surprise, Bhajuratna was given a letter of honour by the Rana Prime Minister Padma Sumsher for his help to the community.

His generous help to the Buddhist monks expelled from Nepal was in later years also honoured by the Buddhist monks themselves. He was chosen to carry the holy Buddhist relic of Sariputramaugalyan in 1951.

The relic was first exhibited in Kalimpong, and at the request of Bhajuratna, it was then also taken to Kathmandu. With great festivity the relic was mounted on a gaily decorated elephant and taken around the city for the benefit of the residents of Kathmandu, with Bhajuratna accompanying the relic. Residents showered the passing relic with rice and flower petals as the procession slowly passed through the narrow lanes of Kathmandu. After several days, the relic was taken back to India.

Bhajuratna was once again honoured by the Buddhist monks when he was chosen to carry the holy *Bodhi pipal* plant presented to the Buddhist of Nepal by the Sri Lankan Buddhists. The Bodhi pipal tree in Sri Lanka is believed to be the sapling of the pipal tree in India under which Buddha gained his enlightenment.

There was another procession around Kathmandu, with Bhajuratna again accompanying the relic. The Bodhi sapling was then planted in front of Anandakuti Vihar in Swoyambhu, by his wife Gyan Maya.

During the Rana regime there was a severe drought in Nepal, which was followed by a famine. This is believed to be after the earthquake. With farmers relying solely on the monsoon rains to plant their paddy, a bad monsoon year followed by another dry year was disastrous for the farmers, resulting in little or no harvest and a shortage of grain in the country. Bhajuratna went to Kathmandu during this period of famine, and to ease the problem of the Nepali people, he imported rice from Burma and had it sold cheaply in the local market.

Bhajuratna keeping in mind his early financially difficult years, donated a substantial sum of money to the *Kasa guthi* – a social organization of the Kansakars. It was an amount that could be borrowed by a fellow Kansakar for his business, and returned to the *guthi* after a couple of years, together with the interest amount as laid down by the *guthi* members.

Bhajuratna donated generously to the *Paropkar* – a social service institute in Kathmandu run by Dayabir Singh Kansakar. To help get it started, Bhajuratna donated several pairs of tailoring scissors, half a dozen sewing machines, and a vehicle.

Since his early young years, Bhajuratna was in the habit of walking to the Guheswari temple in the early hours of the morning, to offer prayers, and he walked home again in the light of dawn. It was a ritual which he tried to keep up even during his prosperous days.

Years later, Bhajuratna had a single storied *satah* built beside the Bishnumati river. It is located between the Pashupati Temple and the Guheswari Temple, and still stands today. A *satah* can be a shelter or house within or outside the city, and is left for charity, to be used by people especially for religious purposes, or even as a shelter. Several *satah*s erected through private funds still exist in and around Kathmandu, especially in street corners, or beside temples.

In the main Guheswari temple itself, Bhajuratna had the gilded pagoda roof of the central temple decorated on all four sides with delicately hanging gilded filigree, and the names of all the family members including grand children embossed along the top edge.

Flourishing Years

In Kalimpong, Bhajuratna bought more property to keep up with his expanding business. 12th May 1939 land was bought at the 10th Mile and a five storied house was built. This building was named Nepali Building. It was used as shops, living quarters for his many employees, and also as a store. 11th January 1940 the *Jyasachhen* – workshop – next to Kanchan cinema hall was bought from Bherulall Parak, and five years later 18th December 1945, the land adjoining the *Jyasachhen* was bought from Fatima Bibi.

The house at Kel Tole belonging to Bhajuratna and his brother Kulratna had been expanded by buying the adjoining houses belonging to Jog Bir Aba and Bhote Baja.

Bhajuratna's little shop cum residence in Kalimpong, on the way down to Hath Bazar had been extended to accommodate his growing family and his expanding business. He now also rented the first floor of the house he lived in. Another house a few blocks away, was also rented which was used as a store and sleeping quarters for some employees, including Dharma Das, Tushi's son, who spent several years in Kalimpong, working for the family. Like everybody else who worked in Kalimpong, he has only fond memories of the years he spent there. One thing he is unable to forget, is having to sleep several nights on piles of silver blocks spread out under his mattress, as there was no space to store them.

By now, most of the Lhasa Newars travelling between Kathmandu and Tibet were lodging at Bhajuratna's house during their short stop over in Kalimpong. The house was popularly called Guhekothi, after the goddess Guheswari.

While Gyan Jyoti was still at Lhasa, Bhajuratna's rented house above Hath Bazar burnt down in 1943. Maniharsha was in Kalimpong, so was able to help his father save some goods from the flames. Gyan Jyoti lost all his medals won for racing during the inter-school competition, and Gyan Maya, Bhajuratna's wife lost everything she possessed. Among other valuables and important documents kept with his wife's belongings, Bhajuratna lost his special letters of honour.

Temporary accommodation for Bhajuratna and his family after the house was destroyed by fire was the Sandu Tshang Building at the 10th Mile. This was located a couple of houses away from the new five storied building which was being used as office, store and living quarters for his many *banjas* – assistants.

In the same year, 5th November 1943 the beautiful old English villa at the 11th Mile was bought, together with the expansive land surrounding it, and the long narrow strip of motorable road leading down the steep hill to the property. The place located below Bhutan House overlooked the Relli River deep down in the valley. A large double storied colonial style stone house, with more than a dozen rooms, a long wide hall on each floor, and a separate building at the back of the house for the kitchen. Also double storied, the kitchen was connected to the main building with a little over-bridge. The house became known to all in Kalimpong as the Bhajuratna Kothi.

A green lawn surrounded the house, with giant magnolia trees growing on both sides of the lawn. On the extensive farm land immediately below the lawn, vegetable was grown for the large household, including millet, corn, and potatoes, onion, garlic, ginger, and turmeric and other seasonal vegetable. And paddy during the monsoon. Down the hill, a good distance from the house was a cow-shed, with space enough for more than a dozen cows. Scores of orange trees grew in the upper and lower flats, and small bamboo forests marked the boundaries of the property. With spring water gushing down the hill in mini waterfalls, there was the endless sound of water to lull one off to sleep, or the cry of the jackal to keep you awake at night.

Most of the *banjas* employed by Bhajuratna whether at Kalimpong, Lhasa or Calcutta were Newars brought from Kathmandu, and very few were hired locally. The cooks were brought from Kathmandu. Several *Jyapus* – Newar farmers of the Kathmandu Valley, from Thimi, Patan and Bhaktapur were employed to work in the farm. It was therefore not unusual for the local employees, whether Nepali, Indian or Tibetan, to pick up the language of the Newars, with some speaking it as fluently as the Newars themselves.

Strange as it may seem, for some *banjas* and most *Jyapus* it was also their first contact with the Nepali language, as the language spoken in Kathmandu was the language of the Newars, where they had little or no contact with the world outside the Kathmandu Valley.

When the King of Bhutan – Raja Dorje's son got married, he celebrated it lavishly with a feast organized for everybody in Kalimpong. A Tibetan merchant was chosen to organize the feast for all the Tibetans, a Marwari for the Marwaris, another person for the Bengalis of Kalimpong, and Bhajuratna was chosen to organize the feast for the Newars.

Bhajuratna's time was divided between Kathmandu, Calcutta and Kalimpong. As the sons took on more responsibility, he had more time to relax and was more often in Kathmandu. Being a religious man, he had the opportunity of visiting different temples in Kathmandu and organising religious ceremonies as often as he wished.

Nevertheless, he always loved being in Kalimpong, where he was able to relax and enjoy the beautiful landscape, the garden full of blossoms, and looking back, be proud of the fruit of his early difficult years, when he had worked hard to keep the family going.

Marriages

With arranged marriages among the Newars of Kathmandu, sons and daughters have no influence over the choice of their future partners. A *lami* – matchmaker – shuttles between the two families, and the only contact the two future in-laws have is through the *lami*. Once the two families have agreed on getting their children married together, *jata* – horoscopes of the future pair are taken to the family astrologer. If they fail to be compatible the *lami* has the task of searching for another prospective bride.

It is the custom among the Newars to go to a *joshi* – astrologer – soon after the birth of a child with the exact date and time of birth. The *joshi* then prepares a life long horoscope for the child, which accompanies him throughout his life. When the person dies, the indispensable *jata* which has also come to the end of its function, is placed by a family member on the lifeless body before cremation, to accompany him into the next world.

Through a *lami* suitable brides were found for Gyan Jyoti and his younger brother Dev Jyoti, born 1932. On 8 July 1946 (BS 2003) the wedding took place. Gyan Jyoti was married to sixteen year old Laxmi Prabha, and Dev Jyoti to eleven year old Tara Devi.

Parents in Kathmandu often married their children very young. However, until they were of age, the young couple did not share a room together. The young bride would sleep with the other daughters of the house and the young husband with his younger brothers. The child bride spent most of her early married years at her *thachhen* – her parents house – and would be regularly summoned by her husband's family for festivals and religious ceremonies. Only after the bride was of the full age of sixteen, would she be permitted to sleep with her husband, and would then also start to permanently live in her husband's house.

Once married, it was quite normal for the young husband to leave his wife with his parents for the first few months, or even the first couple of years of marriage, if business took him away from home.

Laxmi Prabha then sixteen years old remembers those early years at Kel Tole. The child bride Tara Devi was helpless and innocent, and over the next few years in her helplessness grew very attached to her. Still a child, Tara Devi did not know how to wear a sari, and every morning after they woke up, Laxmi Prabha had to help her young sister-in-law get wrapped in her sari. The young brides slept together in one room with Gyan Shova and Hera Shova, the unmarried sisters of their husbands.

Every morning they all went down together to the well to wash themselves, wash clothes, and carry water back for the house. Water was carried by the Newar women on the hip in shining brass *ghas* – water vessels – for their daily cooking, washing and for the toilet. Running water in houses were then still unknown.

Often, when Maniharsha Jyoti and Ratna Jyoti were in Kathmandu on a visit with their wives Keshari Laxmi and Dan Laxmi, their wives also joined the younger sisters-in-law every morning to fetch water from the well. The expanding family often got together in Kathmandu when a religious function was organised by Bhajuratna, or for a family festival, or the feast of the Kasa *guthi* – a social organisation – which takes place annually on the full moon day of February, when all the Kansakars with their families get together for a family feast.

A *guthi* is also a trust or an establishment which manages religious festivals, looks after religious property or charitable funds. A member is obliged to pay a fine if he misses a *guthi* meeting or fails to send a representative from his family. Several *guthis* exist in Nepal, with every Newar family belonging to a *guthi*. It splits the Newars into a number of small groups on the basis of their caste, kin and religion.

Buddhist Pilgrimage

It is not unusual for Newar families to go on pilgrimages, and families do not necessarily have to be rich to undertake such a journey. Some try to go on regular pilgrimages, some make it a once in a life time goal, and others to fulfil a sacred promise after the accomplishment of large undertakings, such as marriages. After the wedding of their two younger sons, Bhajuratna and Gyan Maya undertook a *tirtha yatra* – pilgrimage – to all the Buddhist holy places in India, accompanied by their extended family.

The first pilgrimage had been undertaken two years previously by Bhajuratna and his family after the marriages of their eldest son Maniharsha Jyoti and his cousin Ratna Jyoti. The entourage now included Gyan Jyoti and his wife Laxmi Prabha, Dev Jyoti and his wife Tara Devi, and Bhajuratna's two grown-up unmarried daughters Gyan Shova and Hera Shova.

The pilgrimage started from Thankot, where there was no shortage of transport awaiting the travellers. Groups of porters with their cushioned *doolies* – palanquins – competed with one another to gain customers. Depending on the weight of the traveller, three or four porters carried a person in one doolie, and in this manner they arrived in Bhimphedi. From Bhimphedi a truck transported them on rough bumpy and dusty roads to Amlekgunj, from where they took the narrow gauge train to Birgunj. Next morning in horse drawn carts called *tanga* they travelled to Raxaul, where they boarded the Indian train.

Most part of the pilgrimage was undertaken by train, sometimes bullock-carts were hired, and where available *tangas*. Altogether the pilgrimage lasted almost a month, as long halts were made at each place of worship.

They visited Lumbini, Buddha Gaya, Kushinagar, Saranath, Nalanda, Rajgiri, Ajanta, Ellora including other Buddhist places, and they lodged at Buddhist vihars which had accommodation available for families, where it was possible to do their own cooking.

A conservative man, Bhajuratna stuck strictly to his rituals. Every morning when the train stopped he hurriedly got out and washed himself at the public tap. Water in the train was considered not clean enough. Morning ablution completed, he then had to look for an empty corner to hurriedly say his morning prayers before the train started off again. He refused to eat rice cooked by anybody outside the family, so the female members of the family cooked meals at appropriate stops, while an agitated Bhajuratna insisted on finding a spot where they could have their meals without coming into contact with strangers.

Bhajuratna's choleric temperament marked his character. Those used to him learned to ignore his frequent outbursts, including his bouts of swearing. His dutiful and loyal wife calmly and patiently bore the brunt of his temperament, she learned to get used to her husband's daily explosions in the way we get used to the changing weather.

During the long weeks together, the young brides got closely acquainted with their famous father-in-law. In nervous anxiety they awaited his frequent outbursts, they jumped when he exploded for impatience, they held back tears when their cooking got criticised. Whenever he was in good humour, the young brides were never sure whether his comments were a joke or if he was in earnest. And slowly they learned to adjust themselves to all his likes and dislikes.

The young brides and the young sisters-in-law got along well, they supported and helped each other, they slept together, and like young school girls they giggled and laughed the days and weeks away.

The pilgrimage ended at Bombay, from where Bhajuratna and his family had their first experience with air travel. They flew from Bombay to Calcutta with the two young brides, including Gyan Shova, Hera Shova and Dev Jyoti all travelling as children at half priced tickets. Laxmi Prabha frequently told her children about those early years, how days ahead they were all nervous for excitement, the women especially, thinking about the forthcoming flight. If the men were nervous they managed not to show it.

Would they all be able to travel in one aeroplane? Would they get sick? Would something awful happen to them while they were still up in the sky? What sort of feeling would they have flying in an aeroplane? It was all beyond their wildest imagination. For days due to nervousness, they scarcely had appetite for any food. To the relief of all, the plane ride went smoothly without any mishap, and all were glad when they landed safely and were on firm ground once again.

The group took a few days rest in Calcutta with Maniharsha and his family, where he was handling the family business. From Calcutta, Bhajuratna and his wife Gyan Maya went on to Kathmandu with their two daughters, accompanied by their youngest son Dev Jyoti and his wife. Gyan Jyoti who was responsible for the family business from Kalimpong left with his wife Laxmi Prabha, and returned to Kalimpong.

Ratna Jyoti

In 1944 Kulratna's son, Ratna Jyoti went to Lhasa and took over from Gyan Jyoti as *thakali* of the Syamukapu *kothi* for the next two and a half years, until he was relieved by Gyan Jyoti again.

Gyan Jyoti went to Lhasa for the second time in 1947. This time he was accompanied by his younger brother Dev Jyoti, who was to be introduced into the family trade. After one year working together and teaching his brother the run of the business, Gyan Jyoti returned to Kalimpong, leaving Dev Jyoti as *thakali* of the Lhasa kothi for the next two years.

Ratna Jyoti moved between Kathmandu, Calcutta and Kalimpong, and together with his cousins Maniharsha Jyoti and Gyan Jyoti helped to run the family business.

During his early trip to Lhasa, Ratna Jyoti owned two Tibetan mastiffs, Dhundu and Shandu. When he left Lhasa, the two dogs were brought back with him to Kalimpong. One day, Shandu disappeared from the 11th Mile house. There was a frantic search for him around Kalimpong, all to no avail. A few weeks later, Newar merchants returning from Lhasa brought the news that Shandu was seen in Phari, safe and sound, and very much at home again.

The second dog Dhundu lived for many years in Kalimpong. In contrast to its enormous size, it was mild and patient with the children. It was a good watch dog, became an object of curiosity to the villagers around the 11th Mile due to its unusual size, and prevented people from trespassing.

Ratna Jyoti was preparing to go to Lhasa for the second time, when he died unexpectedly in 1951 in Calcutta after a short illness. He left behind a young wife Dan Laxmi with two small daughters, Siddhi Laxmi and Ganga Shova.

Ratna Jyoti's father Kulratna (Bhajuratna's elder brother) had died several years earlier. As was the custom among the Newars who lived in a joint family, Bhajuratna had taken on the responsibility of financially taking care of his brother's widow Buddhamaya. Now with her son Ratna Jyoti also gone, the young widow Dan Laxmi, and the two small daughters also came under Bhajuratna's care.

Dan Laxmi later moved to Calcutta, to live with Maniharsha Jyoti and his family. Her daughters Siddhi Laxmi and Ganga Shova were sent to schools in Calcutta for a few years, until she returned to settle down in Kathmandu.

His Holiness
The Sixteenth Karmapa

The first contact the Syamukapu family had with the 16th Karmapa Rigpe Dorje was through Gyan Jyoti in 1947, while he was in Tibet for the second time.

The Syamukapu business house in Kalimpong imported Rolex watches from Switzerland which were then re-exported to Lhasa, where they were in great demand. With reasonably high orders for Rolex watches coming from Kalimpong, the Director of the Rolex company in Switzerland wished to visit his importer in India. He arrived in Kalimpong and was astonished to discover that it was but a little village town.

His Holiness the Karmapa wanted a Rolex watch with a golden band. The watch arrived in Lhasa, and not knowing that it was imported for the Karmapa, Gyan Jyoti's younger brother Dev Jyoti started wearing the watch and fancied it for himself. Dev Jyoti was reluctant to part with the watch, even when he learned that it was meant for the Karmapa, and so an embarrassed Gyan Jyoti had to make his excuses with a promise to get another Rolex watch ordered for the Karmapa as soon as possible.

In 1948 while Gyan Jyoti was still at Lhasa, His Holiness the Karmapa visited Kathmandu for the first time. On arriving at Thankot, Kathmandu's entry point, the Karmapa made known his wish to stay at Syamukapu's house. Enquiring along the way as they went, the entourage was directed to Kel Tole, in the heart of Kathmandu.

News spread fast. When the Karmapa reached Kel Tole, Tibetans and Newars were lining the roadside waiting to pay their homage. The long narrow lane leading to the main entrance of *Takhachhen* – big house – as Bhajuratna's house was called, was also thronged by devotees who had heard about the arrival of the Karmapa. They bowed in devotion as he was carried into Bhajuratna's house.

In those early years, when there were no motorable roads over the mountainous terrain leading to Kathmandu, everything required for Kathmandu had to be carried by sturdy porters, including motor cars. It is said that sixty porters were required to transport a motor car on crossed bamboo poles, over the mountain trails to Kathmandu.

Bhajuratna owned a Landrover at this time, which enabled him to take the Karmapa to visit the holy Buddhist temples in and around Kathmandu, the main ones being Swoyambhu and Boudhnath. After some days at Kathmandu, the Karmapa returned to India and from there journeyed back to his Tsurphu monastery in Tibet.

The Karmapa visited Kathmandu for the second time in 1951 with Tokola Rinpoche, and this time too he stayed with Bhajuratna. Gyan Jyoti was always sent a telegram by the Karmapa, before he visited Kalimpong, Calcutta or Kathmandu. And no matter where he was, he always made it a point of travelling there to be present for the Karmapa's visit. Accompanied by Tokola Rinpoche, Chinya Lama and Gyan Jyoti, Karmapa was driven to Swoyambhu the next day, where the existing Tibetan monastery beside the Swoyambhu stupa was offered to His Holiness at a ceremony.

This time when Karmapa left Kathmandu it was by air to Jhapa, a tiny village in east Nepal, accompanied by Tokola Rinpoche and Gyan Jyoti. Despite Lok Darshan Bajracharya's assurance that transport would be arranged for them at Jhapa for their onward journey to the Indian border, there was no transport awaiting them on their arrival. Lok Darshan was then the private secretary to crown prince Mahendra, (King Gyanendra's father).

At Jhapa airfield, Gyan Jyoti managed to hire a *belgari* – bullock cart – for their onward journey, which was loaded with the Karmapa's six boxes of presents, and then with the Karmapa sitting inside the hooded cart, Gyan Jyoti and Tokola Rinpoche walking alongside the *belgari* the tired travellers reached Bhadrapur after an hour or so.

When they got to Bhadrapur, they got in touch with the Dhakwa Sahu who in partnership with Bihari Lal Subbha owned and operated a rice mill in the town. The Dhakwa Sahu was visibly upset and lamented that if he had known he would have sent his car to collect His Holiness and Tokola Rinpoche at the Jhapa airfield. After a rest and a meal, a car was placed at their disposal, and the three set off for the Indian border.

Due to government restrictions, the Nepali car was not permitted to cross into India, and so at the Nepali side of the border, they had to stop their journey. The six boxes of presents were unloaded and placed on the Indian side of the border, on the dusty road side, and the car sent back to Bhadrapur.

Today, unknown to officials, at a remote stretch of road the Indian drivers change the Indian number plates of their jeeps for a Nepali number plate before entering the Nepali border, where they wait to pick up their passengers. Once again in no man's land, back they change into Indian plates before continuing their onward journey to Siliguri.

With the Karmapa resting as comfortably as was possible on one of the boxes, they waited patiently for their next possible transport to Sikkim. How long they would have to wait at this deserted border post, they had no idea.

It was a hot and dusty day. While they waited under the shade of a tree, partly protected from the scorching, sweltering sunshine, an Indian police Jeep drove by, and two policemen stepped out. They were the border police. With the high rate of smuggling on both sides of the border there was a thriving black market in the border villages, hence the presence of the border police.

Noticing the six boxes on the roadside and a Nepali man with two Tibetan travellers, the police were immediately suspicious and demanded to check the boxes.

Gyan Jyoti produced a letter in his possession and handed it over to the police officer. It was a letter from the Indian Foreign Office requesting that all necessary assistance be given to the bearer of the letter. On reading its contents and seeing the Karmapa, a dramatic change over took the over bearing attitude of the police officers. They immediately offered to take the Karmapa and Tokola Rinpoche to Rumtek in their Jeep. Gyan Jyoti was asked to remain with the six boxes to await the local bus transport to Siliguri, from where he could take the next transport to Gangtok, and finally on to Rumtek monastery.

It was one o'clock in the morning when Gyan Jyoti finally arrived at the Rumtek monastery with the six boxes of presents. He remembered seeing the Karmapa looking out of a window, waiting in anxiousness for his arrival at the monastery, and how he smiled with relief as soon as he saw Gyan Jyoti finally arrive safely in the small hours of the morning.

Bhajuratna's Last Days

The Karmapa made his third visit to Kathmandu in December 1956, just two weeks before Bhajuratna died.

Bhajuratna was seriously ill and knew his life was coming to an end. He wrote to his sons about his illness and asked them to return to Kathmandu as soon as possible.

Dev Jyoti the youngest son was in Lhasa again so it was not possible for him to be in Kathmandu when his father died. Gyan Jyoti who was working from Kalimpong left as soon as possible with his wife and three small children to be with his father. Maniharsha Jyoti who was handling business from Calcutta also left for Kathmandu, but annoyed his sick father when he arrived at his father's bed side without his wife and the grandchildren, especially the two grandsons.

This was very important to Bhajuratna, a religious and orthodox man, as together with his two sons, Maniharsha Jyoti and Gyan Jyoti, and their sons Padma Jyoti, Rup Jyoti, and Amrit Jyoti respectively, they would make up the five direct male members of the family who would be required to perform funeral rites after his death.

During this period when Bhajuratna knew his time was nearing, he mentioned to Gyan Jyoti a few times his desire to pay his last respects to the Karmapa. The son's answer was: "How can we request such a high lama to visit Nepal, and at such short notice?"

"It is just my personal wish, do not take it so seriously," would be the sick father's reply.

Another wish that Bhajuratna often expressed some months before he died was his desire to give *bhojan-daan* – donation of food – to monks from all over the world. This seemed to be a wish impossible, but in some strange manner came to be accomplished. In 1956, the same year that Bhajuratna died, the Third World Buddhist Conference was held at Kathmandu, which was participated by many Buddhist monks from almost all parts of the world. Bhajuratna had his long cherished wish fulfilled when he was given the opportunity of offering *bhojan-daan* to the monks during the three days of the conference.

In early December, to Gyan Jyoti's surprise and Bhajuratna's ecstasy, the Karmapa came unannounced to Kathmandu with Tokala Rinpoche and only one servant, and they stayed again at Bhajuratna's house.

For one full week, the Karmapa stayed with the blissfully happy Bhajuratna and slept with him in the same room. No one else was permitted to be present in the room during this period while they prayed and meditated together, except to bring in their meals. After one full week, the Karmapa was ready to leave Kathmandu.

Gyan Jyoti personally drove him down to Raxaul, over the newly constructed north south highway built by the Indian government. The road connected Kathmandu directly to the Indian border town of Raxaul, a seven to eight hour driving distance away.

On arriving at Raxaul railway station, Gyan Jyoti was advised by Karmapa to return immediately to Kathmandu as Bhajuratna did not have very long to live, and so without stopping for a rest, Gyan Jyoti drove back to Kathmandu the same evening.

Within a week of the Karmapa's departure from Kathmandu, Bhajuratna passed away on 20th December 1956.

Bhajuratna's mind was clear right up to the end, but a few things annoyed him. A European doctor from Shanta Bhawan missionary hospital was angrily waved away with impatient gestures much to the embarrassment of a worried Maniharsha. The son wanted to do something good for his father, and so had brought the doctor to see him. Fearing to make the sick man even worse, the doctor made a hasty retreat.

In preparation for his coming death, Bhajuratna sent his younger son Gyan Jyoti to all the main temples around Kathmandu to bring back *parsad* – religious offerings – from the temples of Swyombhu, Boudhanath, Chobar, Guheswari and Sakhu Narayan. While performing a *puja* at Sakhu Narayan, Gyan Jyoti remembered one of the five *kalas* – a water jar used for religious ceremonies – toppling over, much to everybody's consternation. This was not a good omen.

Meanwhile, back at home, the dying Bhajuratna frequently kept inquiring if Gyan Jyoti was back from the temples with the *parsads* for him.

On the day of his death, Bhajuratna was propped up in a sitting position with the help of pillows, as he had wished every day. Thinking that he was tired, members of the family tried to lay him down. This made him angry and they had to hastily prop him up again, which brought back a smile to his face. Several times during the day they tried to make him lie down, but without success. He wished to remain sitting, and in a cross legged position.

It was in this sitting position that he peacefully passed away. Gyan Jyoti believed that he wished to remain sitting so he could meditate reciting the *mantras* given to him by His Holiness the Karmapa.

Almost the whole of the Newar community is believed to have attended Bhajuratna's funeral, including all the Theravada monks of Kathmandu, several Tibetan monks, and several Tibetans residing in Kathmandu, to pay their last tribute to an extraordinary man.

Bhajuratna in the 1950s

Bhajuratna with his grandchildren

1951

Photo taken at the end of the World Buddhist Conference in Kathmandu 1956, with Buddha statues displayed at an alter.

Family Photo-1953

L to R standing: Maniharsha Jyoti with daughter Prabha, Gyan Shova, Hera Shova, Gyan Jyoti with daughter Deb Shova, Dev Jyoti
L to R sitting: Dan Laxmi (Ratna Jyoti's widow) with daughter Ganga Shova, Keshari Laxmi (Maniharsha's wife)with daughter
Poorna Shova,   Buddhi Maya (Bhajuratn's elder brother- Kul Ratna's widow) Siddhi Laxmi (Ratna Jyoti's daughter), Padma Jyoti
(Maniharsha's son) Bhajuratna with Gyan Jyoti's son Amrit Jyoti, Rup Jyoti (Maniharsha's son) wife Gyan Maya, Laxmi Prabha (Gyan
Jyoti's wife) with daughter Dharma Shova, Tara Devi (Dev Jyoti's wife) with daughter Padma Shova.

93

L to R: Maniharsha Jyoti, Padma Jyoti, Bhajuratna, Rup Jyoti, Gyan Jyoti, Amrit Jyoti, Dev Jyoti

Ceremony to celebrate Bhajuratna's appointment as the eldest in the family of the Kansakars – thakalilugu – with the five male members of the family in turban participating in the ceremony.
L to R: Bhajuratna, Maniharsha, Gyan Jyoti, Dev Jyoti and grandson Amrit Jyoti who has taken off his white turban

With Ananda Kaushalyan Bhikkhu of India

With Narad Bhikkhu of Sri Lanka

Wife Gyan Maya

Meeting of Theravada monks at the Bhajuratna Kothi in Kalimpong, with Narad Bhikkhu of Sri Lanka (next to Bhajuratna in white cap) to plan on approaching the Rana government in Nepal to abrogate their exile law against the Buddhist monks. Also seen in the picture sitting to the far right is Amritananda Bhikkhu of Kathmandu.

Front view of house at Shreegha Vihar, which was built and donated to the Thervada monks by Bhajuratna

Below L & R: Prayers held beside the newly donated building at Shreegha Vihar

The Buddhist relic of Sariputramaugalyan –1951

Due to his religious activities and his support to Buddhism, Bhajuratna was on several occasion selected by the Theravada Order to carry Buddhist relics around Kathmandu. The photo on this page including the following photos show him executing these special honours.

Bhajuratna receiving the Bodhi Plant from Narad Bhikkhu at the start of a procession

On the way to Anandkuti Vihar Swoyambhu, with the Bodhi Plant which was later planted by his wife Gyan Maya in front of Anandkuti Vihar

At Anandkuti Vihar with the Bodhi Plant

Bhajuratna going around Kathmandu on an elephant, with a Buddhist relic

100

An Astidhatu – relic – from Swoyambhu being taken around Kathmandu. Bhajuratna is to the left on the carriage, dressed in white, holding the relic. In the past, it was taken around Kathmandu every three years

King Tribhuvan of Nepal with Theravada monks. To the far right is Mahanam Bhikkhu of Kathmandu.

Bhajuratna with Lhasa Newars and children in Kalimpong during the Dasain festival

*Amritnanda Bhikkhu with King Tribhuvan and
Crown Prince Mahendra at the Anandakuti Vihar, Kathmandu.*

*Photo taken on the occasion of the Buddhist Mahaparitran ceremony, held at the
Naranhity Palace. Seen in the picture is King Tribhuvan*

Bhajuratna with Theravada monks at Anandakuti Vihar, Kathmandu.

Bhajuratna, wife Gyan Maya and daughter Gyan Shova with Theravada monks at Nalanda, India

Theravada monks of Nepal

Standing L to R: 1. Dharmalok Bhikkhu 2. Mahanam Bhikkhu, 3, 4 & 5 n/n
Sitting L to R: Sudharshan Bhikkhu and Amritananda Bhikkhu

Dec. 1956 – Two weeks before Bhajuratna succumbed to his illness, the Karmapa arrived unexpectedly in Kathmandu with only one servant and Tokola Rinpoche, and spent a week alone with Bhajuratna. Also seen in the photo are son Gyan Jyoti and wife Gyan Maya

Bhajuratna with the Karmapa two weeks before he died

Children from L to R: Padma Shova, Dharma Shova,
Amrit Shova, Amrit Jyoti and Deb Shova

*Maniharsha Jyoti and Gyan Jyoti clad in white according to local custom.
Picture taken a few minutes before the pyre was lighted*

The Syamukapu Kothi, Lhasa

L to R: The old Phari Kothi and the renovated Phari Kothi

Part Two

Gyan Jyoti's Early Years

Gyan Jyoti was a quiet man, shy by nature and unlike his father rarely lost his temper. He was the type who expressed his happiness, his pride and affection in silence. He was honest, open and soft hearted, a nature which in later years when the family grew apart, was his greatest disadvantage. However, it was this very nature, this honesty and openness that won him trust, respect and affection from people of all social levels, from people he came into contact with in the course of his life time.

Gyan Jyoti was born on 24th January 1921 at Kel Tole, shortly after midnight at 12:35. He was the first child of Gyan Maya Tuladhar, Bhajuratna's second wife, and was followed by three sisters. The eldest died as a child, then came Gyan Shova, Hera Shova, and a brother twelve years his junior, Dev Jyoti.

As earlier described, four *kalighars* – handworkers – travelled to Kalimpong from Kathmandu accompanied by Bhajuratna's wife and their four year old son Gyan Jyoti. He now had the opportunity of going to school like all the other children, and was immediately admitted into the kindergarten section of the Girl's High School, run by the Scottish Mission.

111

As soon as he was older, he was admitted into the Scottish Universities Mission Institute (SUMI) for boys. From then on, the next forty years were mostly spent in Kalimpong.

The Scottish Mission started its work in Kalimpong in 1873. It founded a hospital in the missionary compound, built a leper colony, and separate High Schools for boys and girls. SUMI was established in 1887, the year that Rev.W.Macfarlane, a missionary of the Church of Scotland died suddenly at the age of forty seven. Macfarlane was the founder of several schools scattered around the areas of Darjeeling and Kalimpong. He initiated the building of the church in Kalimpong, but he never lived long enough to see the finish of the church that bears his name. The steepled church is today an integral part of the Kalimpong skyline.

After the Buddhist monks were expelled from Nepal in 1926 and 1944, Kalimpong became a focal point for Buddhist monks due to the generosity of the Newar traders living in Kalimpong. It was said that the most outstanding benefactor among them all was Bhajuratna Kansakar.

Gyan Jyoti's early years were influenced by the Mahayana and Theravada monks his father was supporting, and who were frequently in and out of Bhajuratna's house. Gyan Jyoti was only five years old when Guru Tshering Norbhu arrived in Kalimpong in 1926, on his way to Tibet. He was accompanied by his followers, the five expelled Mahayana monks of Nepal. The monks received their daily meals at Bhajuratna's house. They were so well looked after, that their initial intention of staying in Kalimpong for only a few days, was extended to eight months.

Guru Tshering Norbhu was very fond of having Gyan Jyoti sitting on his lap while he said his prayers. When his mother brought in the meal for the Guru and his monks, he had to stand up to offer the monks their meal. This was Gyan Jyoti's daily routine, offering meals prepared by his mother to the monks, recitation of *panchaseel* – the five Buddhist precepts for lay people – and listening to Buddhist stories. And often he was told that serving ones parents is one of the noblest deeds in life.

His other early introduction to Buddhism was then through Dharmaditya Dharmacharya who arrived in Kalimpong some weeks after Guru Tshering Norbhu and his monks had departed for Tibet. On learning that Gyan Jyoti and his brothers were being sent to the Scottish missionary school, he approached Bhajuratna and told him that his sons would become Christians if they continued being educated in the missionary school, and offered to educate them himself.

In the Buddhist Library opened by Dharmaditya Dharmacharya, Gyan Jyoti started receiving a Buddhist education, which included daily meditation and *panchaseel* prayers. After a couple of years of Buddhist schooling, Gyan Jyoti went back to the Scottish Missionary School when Dharmaditya Dharmacharya went to live in Calcutta. In later years, Gyan Jyoti was also influenced by Mahapragya Bhikkhu (one of the five Mahayana monks expelled from Nepal). Influenced by the teachings of Dharmaditya Dharmacharya, Mahapragya on his return from Tibet had converted to Theravada Buddhism, and continued to practise Buddhism in Kalimpong for several years.

In 1934 Pandit Rahul Sankrityayan, who later became a well known Buddhist scholar, came to Kalimpong before undertaking his second journey to Tibet. At this time, he was still a Bhikkhu, and Bhajuratna had undertaken to sponsor his trip to Lhasa. Until his day of departure, Pandit Rahul Sankrityayan who later mastered seven languages, lived in

Bhajuratna's house. Gyan Jyoti was often in and out of his room, and everytime he saw the monk, he was always writing. Even when ill, Pandit Rahul Sankrityayan would be lying in bed and writing.

One day when Gyan Jyoti returned home from school, the Pandit called him into his room and asked him to sketch for him on paper the *karuwa* – water vessel – on his table. The older man was very pleased to see the finished sketch and later said to Bhajuratna: "Your son is very observant and hardworking. Next year when I come back from Tibet, I plan to go to Japan, I would like to take your son to Japan with me, and I will have him educated there. Please give me your son."

Bhajuratna was unwilling to part with his son, and Rahul Sankrityayan went alone to Japan in 1935, where he stayed for some years learning the Japanese language and familiarising himself with Buddhism in Japan.

When India got her independence from the British in 1947, the Indians were left with a native language that lacked technical vocabulary. Pandit Rahul Sankrityayan who by then had given up his monastic life, was given the task by Prime Minister Jawaharlal Nehru of compiling an English to Hindi technical dictionary. For two years, supported by Bhajuratna's family, he lived in Kalimpong, and with the help of a Professor for English, a Professor for Sanskrit, and a typist, he worked on the assignment.

On the occasion of Dr. Rahul's birthday, in 1949 a party was organized by Gyan Jyoti at the Bhajuratna Kothi, 11th Mile, to which were invited many high ranking people of Kalimpong, Bhutan and Tibet.

Mahapandit Rahul Sankrityayan, or Professor Rahul as he was also called, lived in Calcutta after he had given up his monastic life. After his marriage to a Nepali woman, he left Calcutta and settled down in Darjeeling. Many years later, when Gyan Jyoti visited him in Darjeeling, he was suffering from an illness and had lost much of his memory. His wife then had the sorrowful task of trying to teach him to read and write. Professor Rahul was also unable to recognize his visitor. It was a tragic end for a man once so intellectually active all his life.

Education at Home

From his early years, young Gyan Jyoti received a strict and disciplined upbringing from his father Bhajuratna. A hardworking, simple and honest man, he expected his children to grow up with these same values. As soon as Gyan Jyoti was able to read and write, he was given little tasks by his father.

Every evening Gyan Jyoti and his cousin Ratna Jyoti (son of Bhajuratna's brother) were made to count the days income and write down the cash balance. Often the boys would have to double check, as the balance would not be correct, then approach Bhajuratna to mention the missing amount. Sometimes the answer would be : "Oh yes, I took some rupees for buying grocery," or "I gave a beggar a few paisas," which would then add up to the correct balance. Sometimes it would be: "Yes, I simply forgot, I still have a few rupees in my pocket which I have to put into the cash box."

Someday it happened that the young cousins wanted to finish their counting quickly so they could go play or do their school work and closed up their counting saying the cash balance was correct even though a couple of rupees or a few paisas would be missing, hoping that they would get away with their little lie.

"What! *beeman masta,* – dishonest children, – how can the balance be correct when I still have some rupees in my pocket which I have to put into the cash box. Children, count again, there must be a mistake!" and so they would have to start all over again. The boys realised that it was always better to be honest, even when they found more money in the box, because Bhajuratna often either added or removed money to check their honesty.

Goods brought into Kalimpong from the low lying plains of Calcutta were copper and brass sheets for workshops in Kalimpong, rice, barley and spices and other general merchandise. In those early years, goods were transported via railway to Giellekhola station, down below in the plains. From Giellekhola they arrived in Kalimpong over a ropeway system located just below the wool godowns at Topkhana, and the location continued being called *ghirling* in much later years, even after the ropeway system had come to a standstill.

From the ropeway station, goods were transported to the various Kalimpong merchants by bullock cart. The end station for goods such as wool, yak tail and Tibetan block tea among other goods arriving by mule or donkey caravan from Tibet, was the present day Motor Stand. The animals were grazed in the fields just below the present day *mela- ground –* fair ground.

Every morning, young Gyan Jyoti had to be in school at eight o'clock, but very often he would be late. *Baku* – loads, bales, bundles and boxes of goods – for Bhajuratna seemed to arrive in Kalimpong only in the early mornings, just when he had to leave for school. Bhajuratna would say to him: "Go check how much *baku* has arrived for me." Disobeying an elder was unheard of, so he did what was asked of him. "What do they contain?" The boy had not been asked to see what the *bakus* contained, but without a word of complaint he would run back to check again. Only when his father was satisfied with all the information he needed, the boy would be allowed to run to school.

Gyan Jyoti was anxious not to be late for school, he therefore started noting down precise details when checking the arrival of goods. His angry protests to the muleteers to bring goods into Kalimpong either earlier or later during the day as he had to go to school fell on deaf ears. It was very annoying, but there was nothing he could do about it, and there was a simple unwritten law that the young obey the elder, especially if that elder was ones own father.

Raw material required for Bhajuratna's metal workshop was ordered from Calcutta, so another task that Gyan Jyoti was often made to do was to run to Tharchin Babu of Ladhak, to either get a letter translated or written for his father. Tharchin Babu was a Christian, an educated man who could read and write in English.

Every time a letter arrived for Bhajuratna, either Gyan Jyoti or Ratna Jyoti would be sent to Tharchin Babu to get it translated. If his father was not satisfied with the translation, or the letter was not according to his expectation, the response would be, "Either you did not understand what he said, or Tharchin Babu is a bad translator. Go back and ask him to translate the letter once more!"

Tharchin Babu rebuked the boy when he had to translate the letter all over again, as the very thing Bhajuratna wanted to know had already been explained to the youngster earlier, "Child, be more attentive next time!" would be the stern reproach. And the next time the boy concentrated on every word, even though he did not understand what the words meant.

Gyan Jyoti remembered all the running he did, running on daily errands for his father and daily running late to school, but all this running was not in vain.

On the occasion of King George V of England's Silver Jubilee in 1935, there was an inter-school sport contest organised in Kalimpong at the *mela-ground*. It was also Kalimpong's annual football stadium, and a place for every other happening as is still today. Gyan Jyoti won five medals in all for various races he participated in during the twenty days of contest, however all this happened without the knowledge of his father.

In the following days, Bhajuratna got to learn from various merchants how good his son was in running and how he had won several medals at the recent inter-school sporting contest. Bhajuratna was advised to give his son plenty of milk to drink so he would remain a strong runner. Ever since then, the proud father made Gyan Jyoti drink a daily glass of milk before leaving for school so that he would continue being a strong runner.

Kayta Puja

In 1930, accompanied by his mother and cousin Ratna Jyoti, Gyan Jyoti went to Kathmandu to go through the *kayta puja* – ceremonial rite for young boys – and to receive his *nikha* – prayer beads. They travelled to Calcutta first, to Maniharsha, who was at the time living with Dhamma Sahu at his business house in Calcutta. Maniharsha was preparing for his school examination around this period, so was unable to accompany his family to Nepal. Unable to persuade Maniharsha to travel with them, they finally left without him.

While in Kathmandu, Gyan Jyoti's mother and her sister-in-law Buddha Maya, started arrangements for marrying Laxmi Hera (her step daughter), and niece Dev Prabha (the daughter of Bhajuratna's elder brother Kulratna and Buddha Maya) and got in touch with a *lami* – a matchmaker. According to the Newar custom, it is inappropriate for families to get into direct contact with the concerned family, when searching for a suitable bride for their sons. While his mother was busy every day with the *lami* to finalise marriage agreements, Gyan Jyoti was left alone at home at Kel Tole to prepare meals.

This was one of those periods when he missed having his mother around, and realized that cooking was not as easy as it seemed. In later years he laughed about it, remembering the many mishaps to his cooking. The *dal* – lentil soup – getting burnt everyday, the rice never being right, and his mother pretending to enjoy the meals prepared by her nine year old son with the consoling words, *"Saa babu,"* – tastes good boy.

According to another Newar custom, a father is necessary to perform the religious ceremony of *kanya daan* – giving away of daughter – at a wedding.

Bhajuratna had earlier left his work in Kalimpong and travelled to Kathmandu to marry off his elder two daughters Gyan Prabha and Laxmi Prabha from his first marriage, and to perform the *kanya daan* for them. With his elder brother Kulratna gone, and the children all still young, Bhajuratna had the extra burden of earning money for the large joint family. When his third daughter was to get married, he was unable to leave Kalimpong again due to work pressure. It would have meant another long journey to Nepal, and several days away from work which he could not afford.

Therefore when the time came two years later, for the wedding of Laxmi Hera, his third daughter from his first marriage, and Kulratna's daughter Dev Prabha, Gyan Jyoti was made to accompany his mother to Kathmandu. Representing his father at the age of eleven, he performed the *kanya daan* for them and sat through all the long marriage ceremonies.

Buying Brocade in Benaras

Gyan Jyoti's schooling was interrupted very often. His father knew the importance of education, but believed the purpose of education had been achieved when a child could read, write and count.

This time he was to go to Benaras to buy *tinkha* – brocade – for his father, accompanied by Ratna Tamrakar, a *banja* – assistant – known to the family as Nati *Paju* or maternal uncle. Benaras was in those years renowned for its rich silk, gold and silver brocade work, woven by many Muslim families. With great pride Gyan Jyoti often mentioned to his children that he was only fourteen or fifteen years old when he was first sent to Benaras by his father, to buy brocade.

From Siliguri, Gyan Jyoti and Nati *Paju* took the train to Benaras. They were to head for Udogpura, but on arriving at the Benaras railway station they were unable to proceed further to their destination as no one seemed to have ever heard of the place called Udogpura. The boy directed the hired *tanga* – horse carriage – to take them to the post office, the best people to ask for directions. As expected, one of the post office employees instructed them to head for Pilli Kothi, which was the local name for Udogpura.

The two brocade merchants of Benaras known to Bhajuratna were Niyam Tulla Nizam Uddin, a not very successful merchant, and the rich Haji Kasim Haji Mohamed Isaz. These two brocade merchants were also contacts for the other Lhasa Newars of Kalimpong. When the Newars were in Benaras, they all lodged at Haji Kasim's house.

During the day Gyan Jyoti received his instructions on all aspects of brocade under the guidance of Niyam Tulla. He was given an insider knowledge on everything dealing with brocade, was taught what he should look for in good quality brocade and what he should avoid. Powered with this knowledge and all the good advice still fresh in his mind, Gyan Jyoti went around to the brocade dealers to place his orders.

A wide range of brocade was placed before him to choose from. It was a challenging task, but he went through them all slowly, examined each one and set some aside. Finally he made his choice, picking out only the best for his father. A few days later, an order for ten thousand rupees worth of high quality brocade had been placed, to be delivered to Kalimpong. Business accomplished, Gyan Jyoti and Nati *Paju* prepared for their journey home.

On the day of departure a surprise awaited them. The brocade dealers he had come into contact with during his stay in Benaras, had come to say farewell to this unusual young boy who knew so much about their brocade trade. They came with flower garlands while the women standing around the courtyard threw flowers on him. Soon he could barely see due to all the garlands piling up his face.

Gyan Jyoti was touched, and felt happy to be so honoured. Finally accompanied by two of the brocade merchants to the railway station, he was seen off as a very special guest of honour.

It was only at the age of twenty, that Gyan Jyoti could finally complete his schooling. He went to Calcutta to do his final year, his matriculation. In 1942 he sat for his matriculation examination in Darjeeling, and before returning to Kalimpong, he registered himself for admission into college in Darjeeling. Unfortunately, his desire to join college could not be realised, as his father sent him to Lhasa, the same year that he finished schooling.

Preparation for Lhasa

To fulfil his father's promise to Hera Ratna, Gyan Jyoti finally agreed to go to Lhasa to take over the Syamukapu *kothi* as *thakali* – head – although he had already registered himself for college. The auspicious day for Gyan Jyoti's departure for Lhasa was fixed. It was to be 6th December 1942.

A *Bhinapuja* – an elaborate religious ceremony to pray for a traveller's safe journey – was performed for Gyan Jyoti's forthcoming and first journey to Tibet. Preparations had to be made for this long and dangerous journey. Warm clothes had to be stitched, others who were to accompany him had to be informed and also prepared for the journey.

Bhajuratna advised his son to go and pay his respects to Raja Dorjee (King of Bhutan) and to Panda Tshang, the Governor of Yatung, or Dhumo as known to the Tibetans, a Tibetan town which lies halfway between Gangtok and Phari.

The Bhutan royal family has a house at the 11th Mile called Bhutan House, frequently used by its royal members. It must be kept in mind that Kalimpong was once the headquarter of the Bhutan Government until 1865. Although Kalimpong now belonged to British India, the Bhutanese royal family continued owning Bhutan House, perhaps due to a special agreement with the British Government. And with Kalimpong once being the seat of the Bhutan Government it continued being the permanent home of their Queen Mother.

Bhajuratna's close contact with the Bhutan royal family had grown due to his business dealings with them. He now wished that his son out of respect take leave from them before his departure for Tibet.

Raja Dorjee was horrified and annoyed to hear what Gyan Jyoti had come to tell him, "Impossible! You cannot travel to Lhasa at this time of the year. Your father cannot be in his right mind! Do you want to die of cold on the way to Lhasa?"

"No, no, Raja Sahib, nothing will happen to me," replied the young visitor. "My father has already offered prayers for my safe journey, and the astrologers say 6th December is an auspicious time of the year for me to make this journey."

Rani Dorjee who was also in the room smiled as she listened to them. In the course of their conversation, King Dorjee turned to Rani Dorjee and asked her if she had warm *docha* – Tibetan boots – to give the boy for his journey. The queen was soon back in the room with a new pair of boots in-lined with sheep wool. As Gyan Jyoti left with his royal present, both Raja Dorjee and Rani Dorjee wished him a safe journey.

Gyan Jyoti's next visit was to Panda Tshang, the Governor of Yatung, who lived partly in Kalimpong where he owned a large house. He was just as horrified and unwilling to believe that this young boy was being sent to Lhasa in the middle of winter. Gyan Jyoti started all over again to pacify him too with his explanation about his father's *pujas* for his safe journey and how it was to be an auspicious day to start on the journey.

Panda Tshang offered to send his brother-in-law Jhambala to accompany him on his journey to Lhasa. Before he left the house, Gyan Jyoti was presented with a pair of goat skin trousers in-lined with wool, and with much misgiving the older man wished him a safe journey.

On the day of departure Gyan Jyoti received from his mother the auspicious *saga(n)* – a traditional gift of boiled eggs and roasted fish offered as symbols of good luck. A Newar rite appropriate for all occasion, this time as a farewell act.

He was accompanied by Heraratna's younger brother, cousin Dev *dai* – elder brother – Hari Bahadur Shrestha, Jetha Tamang, Kalu Tamang and Jhambala, with his father's final advice *"Ek ka double, sau ka sawai"* – a business man's simple motto, not quite simple to translate into one English sentence. A man who sells his ware at twice its rate will make profit only for that one item he is able to sell. However, if he sells it for a small profit, the income he earns from it will be a hundredfold as he will be successful in selling not just one item but a hundred.

His father's sound advice accompanied Gyan Jyoti not just in Tibet but throughout his life.

Journey to Lhasa

The journey from Kalimpong to Lhasa which normally took at least twenty-five days was on this occasion undertaken in eight days. From Kalimpong, the party travelled to Gangtok by jeep. The same day they were driven to the 15th Mile, where there were people waiting for them with horses and mules. Everything they required for the long journey was packed onto the mules, and without wasting further time, they started off.

From the 15th Mile, riding on mules they passed through the Nathula Pass to Yatung where they stayed for two days. With fresh animals they continued to Phari, where they made a halt for the day.

Phari was a desolate village, a Tibetan trade post where the Himalayan foothills ended and the Tibetan plateau began. The Newar traders on their way to Lhasa were happy when they managed to get to Phari safely, as at Phari, they had the worst part of the journey behind them.

Their animals were changed again for the next step of the journey. They rode on to Dhwila, next Kalapantam then Gyantse. Before Gyantse, the travellers made a one day stop instead of the regular two days. From Gyantse to Lhasa with fresh animals again, they made it in three days.

At every halt, with Jhambala, Panda Tshang's brother-in-law accompanying them on the journey, the travellers were treated with great respect. They were given special attention everywhere they arrived, as they were guests of Panda Tshang, the Governor of Dhumo. They were welcomed with hot Tibetan tea and warm meals, and after a rest, refreshed they continued their journey.

Gyan Jyoti remembered little of the journey except for the fact that it was cold all the time, and the landscape was monotonous, dismal and barren every day. As far as the eyes could see, there was nothing but snow, and then in the middle of no where a poor looking village with a few houses.

Jhambala's elder brother was head Lama of Dhepung Gumbha, which they passed on their way to Lhasa. Here they made a halt while the lamas offered *puja* for the travellers. They were given a warm meal before they were allowed to continue their journey.

Finally, they arrived safely in the outskirts of Lhasa. Here the Syamukapu *banjas* were waiting to welcome them with *khadas* – white silk scarves – and food for the travellers. After some refreshment, they all made their way to a monastery where the travellers offered *khadas* at the shrine of Buddha as thanksgiving for their safe arrival, and then they were led to the Syamukapu *kothi*.

The Tibetan way

It is astonishing how travellers to and from Lhasa found their way over strange barren landscape. When Gyan Jyoti was asked how they ever managed to find their way without maps and compasses, the simple answer was, they did not know the way, they trusted the mules to take them to their destination. There was no questioning the matter, the mules knew where to go.

A yak tail dyed in red was tied on to the lead mule's head, and the rest of the animals followed him. Selected mules were given turns during the journey in wearing the red head gear. As soon as an animal was given the red yak tail, it instinctively knew what its responsibility was, and the other animals also seemed to know exactly what to do, they followed the new leader.

There was an unwritten tradition among the Tibetans regarding pack mules and yaks, which was strictly observed by all Tibetans. Once a year, for one full month, pack animals were given a break, an actual holiday. The animals did no work for a month, carried no loads at all, and spent a month grazing, sleeping, getting fat and regaining their lost energy for the coming months of hard labour.

Tibetans smelled different. Due to the scarcity of water, they rarely washed themselves. *Champa* – roasted barley flour – was their staple diet, it was eaten kneaded into dough with Tibetan butter tea, a drink which can actually taste nice if the butter is not rancid. The soft *champa* was also used to clean their long thick Tibetan robe. Rubbed between the hands the soft *champa* dough removed dirt, and both grownups and children had their faces rubbed with *champa* to keep them clean. And all day long, between meals they drank non-stop butter tea to keep themselves warm. Plates were seldom washed after meals, they were either licked clean or cleaned with paper if there was any available.

When somebody died, he received a sky burial, he was neither buried nor burned, but fed to the vultures in an area out of town. A special class of low caste Tibetans undertook the unpleasant task of chopping up the corpse and throwing it in pieces to the hungry birds.

Tibetan brothers shared one wife, it was quite normal, and seemed not to have caused friction in the family. It was often the case, that only one brother would be left in the house, as the others would be permanently on the move either working or looking for work. If the wife had a brother in her room, his shoes would be discreetly placed outside the room, a sign that they be left undisturbed. The wish was respected by all the others.

If money was needed in a hurry by a merchant, they were given unnumbered fresh bank notes from the mint. This was then to be taken to an artist, who then hand painted the final serial numbers that were missing.

Newar merchants who were leaving Lhasa at the end of their working term, walked in a procession to the Buddhist monasteries, to place their *khadas* at the shrines for the last time, and to pray for their safe journey home. This was also an opportunity for those remaining behind to know who was leaving the country, and to use the opportunity to make claims against anybody planning to leave without clearing their unpaid debts.

A son from every Tibetan family, and often even a daughter would be offered to live as a monk or nun in one of the many Buddhist monasteries around Tibet. In this manner, monasteries then received life long support from their family members. This explains the large number of monks found in every monastery in those early years prior to the Chinese occupation.

Once a year, a traditional event took place peculiar only to Tibet. There was a month long period called Monlam, around February, when the administration of Lhasa was handed over to the Lamas, when the head Lamas of monasteries in Lhasa became the rulers of Lhasa. They had the say, were in charge of all executive functions of Lhasa, and all levies collected which were due to the state during this period was used in the maintenance of monasteries.

During this period of Monlam, the monks were responsible for seeing that the folks kept the city clean. Monastery guardians, big ferocious looking Tibetans walked around the town with their long big sticks, collecting fines from owners of shops and houses if their surroundings were not clean and orderly. People had to be dressed in a presentable manner, and women had to keep their hair braided.

For the rest of the year it was quite normal that every governing body had a Lama as head of the ministry.

A Miraculous Recovery

Gyan Jyoti had been a vegetarian since his childhood, and some weeks after arriving in Lhasa he fell seriously ill. There were no doctors near and wide, but Jog Muni Shakya of Sankhu Nepal, a *baidya* – a spiritual healer with knowledge of ayurvedic medicine – tended to the young *Sahu's* illness. From the conversations going on around him, Gyan Jyoti who was too weak to talk or to keep his eyes open, understood that his time was coming to an end.

Jog Muni Shakya took the sick *Sahu's* pulse and after a few minutes told those in the room that they would have to wait and watch until 5 p.m. in the evening. Assuming that Gyan Jyoti was not able to hear them any more, he told them not to buy fresh meat for the day and to inform the other Newars too.

According to Newar tradition, after a death in a family, those close to the deceased must refrain from eating meat. For relatives of the deceased, it is the first seven days from the official thirteen days of mourning. For others it is three days. Here in Lhasa, hundreds of miles away from home and family, the Newars were, where traditional customs were concerned, closely united and lived like a large extended family, and so together they mourned and respected the loss of a fellow Newar.

Gyan Jyoti remembered trying to open his weary eyes, trying to focus them with effort on a picture hanging in front of him in the room. He thought the picture looked unusual, it seemed to be hanging upside down. Recalling Jog Muni *guruju's* words to those in the room, he remembered thinking sadly about his parents and the purpose of this trip to Lhasa, his two year responsibility as *thakali* of their *kothi*. He recalled severely telling himself that he could not and must not die without first fulfilling his parents wishes. Gyan Jyoti was in later years firmly convinced that it was this strong will power to live on, to complete the task he was sent to Lhasa for, which gave him the energy, a supernatural power to fight for his life.

Harilal, his *banja* – assistant – came to him and whispered into his ears, "*Sahu*, would you like some horlicks?" Gyan Jyoti barely managed to move his head in assent and was given two spoons of warm sweet horlicks to sip. Slowly he felt the warmth return into his body and gradually he felt the energy seeping into him.

After a few more sips of horlicks, he looked at the picture hanging in front of him again. As he continued staring at the picture, to his astonishment, very slowly, it turned until finally it was not upside down anymore. This was unusual, a spiritual sign for him alone, and he knew now he was out of danger.

Faithful Harilal continued feeding his Sahu with spoonfuls of horlicks at frequent intervals, and with each spoonful Gyan Jyoti felt himself regaining a little more energy.

Everyone said their *Sahu* had made himself weak and ill because he was a vegetarian and would not touch meat. Even during his convalescence he continued being a vegetarian, and so was given to drink plenty of soup. After one full month of being in bed and with everybody taking good care of him,

Gyan Jyoti could once again continue with the work he had come to Lhasa to undertake.

Purna Dhar Tuladhar visited Gyan Jyoti regularly while he was bed-ridden, and kept him company out of gratitude for the recent help he had received. Purna Dhar was at the time going through a difficult phase in Lhasa, he was financially down, had nothing to sell in his shop and had gone to Gyan Jyoti for help.

Gyan Jyoti who had loads of matches in his storeroom advised Purna Dhar to fill his show cases with all the match boxes available, which he could remove when he had other material to sell in his shop. He did as he was advised. At least his shop was now not empty, and as weeks and months went by, and with some financial help, he was slowly able to replace the match boxes filling the shelves with other merchandise.

Purna Dhar Tuladhar never forgot the incident. He always remained grateful and tried to help in anyway he could. He was a very good *kastu* – musk – expert, and he used his expertise to later regularly buy high quality musk for Gyan Jyoti.

The Bhajuratna *kothi* at Lhasa was more popularly known to all as the Syamukapu *kothi*. This was located at Jhyalinchokam on the main street called Barkor where almost all the other Newars had their shops including the *khacharas* – the offsprings of Newar men and Tibetan women. There was a big *bahi* or *viha*r – temple – built by the earlier Newars, from where the streets led in different directions. It was also called the Singha Sartha Aju's stupa, who is known to the Tibetans as Norbhu Sangya.

The Syamukapu *kothi* was located close to this *vihar* and alongside the back of the building was located the local police station and jail. From the terrace of the Syamukapu *kothi* the prisoners in the yard below could be observed baring their bottom as they bent to be whipped as punishment.

One time a woman is said to have taken the place of her husband after she had helped him to escape, and so there was much agitation when the man in charge of whipping the prisoners was confronted with a woman's bared bottom. The woman was of course made to leave the prison premises immediately. There were also occasions when one or two prisoners managed to escape from the prison yard, by digging beneath the walls, and to flee via the Syamukapu *kothi*.

The Newars in Lhasa

In Tibet, the Lhasa Newars organized *guthis* for themselves, which were referred to as *palas*. There were seven of them. These *palas* organized all the festivals and feasts as observed in Nepal, and so hundreds of miles away from home and their family, the Newars were able to continue their tradition and culture.

The Lhasa Newars celebrated all their Newar festivals with great enthusiasm, two of them being *Mohani* – the Hindu Dasain festival between September and October, and *Sunti* – the Tihar, the festival of lights, between October and November. *Sunti* is more important as it marks the Newar new year, when all business houses close their old accounts and start the new year with new ledger books blessed by Laxmi, the Hindu goddess of wealth.

The Newar Buddhists are *vajrayanis* a mixture of Hinduism and Buddhism peculiar to Nepal, and therefore it is not unusual and quite understandable if outsiders are unable to distinguish where one religion begins and where the other ends.

Most Newar traders stayed only two to three years in Lhasa until they were replaced by a brother or a relative, others stayed on for longer period, and all learnt to speak Tibetan fluently. Away from home and family, many Newars although already married with wife and children back home, had Tibetan wives who bore them children in Tibet. Some women followed their men to Nepal, but many were left behind.

The Newars liked to remain within their little circle. If there was business to discuss which called for a meeting among the Newar traders, the Newar *sahus* instead of personally attending often sent their *banjas* who were not in a position to make decisions. The Tibetans took advantage of this lack of communication among the Newars, when buying or selling goods to them, which finally inspired some of the young Newars to form an organisation to counteract this problem.

In 1943, in collaboration with the young Lhasa Newars, the Lhasa Nepal Chamber of Commerce was established. It was during the period when Kesar Bahadur Bista, the Nepali government's political agent for Tibet was still in Lhasa. Gyan Jyoti was made it's vice president for proposing this co-operation, and it was agreed that profit from their business be put into the committee to specially help Newars with financial problems, and those not having the means enough to return to Nepal.

The Chamber of Commerce had to be dissolved in 1944 due to pressure from the Newar elders in Calcutta who feared that the youngsters in Lhasa were not in their right minds. An order to dissolve this chamber was sent to Lhasa via telegram signed by seven Newar elders. The order was therefore promptly obeyed by its young members.

Many of the Newars living in Lhasa participated in an annual eight day festival cum trade fair held at the ancient village of Jampaling, which required a three days travel from Lhasa. This took place in the sixth Tibetan month, which fell around July or August. Nomads and traders from bordering areas participated in the fair, including Tibetan villagers from far and near. The Newars were there some days ahead of the fair to make preparations for the religious ceremony.

This festival is believed to be centuries old and is said to have been started by Singha Sartha Aju of Kathmandu, in whose honour a shrine was built in the Newar style. According to this ancient tradition, trading at the fair could not begin until a 165 meter long strip of consecrated cloth called *pata* was unfurled from the top of the huge stupa, located at the centre of the village. This was initiated by the old Newars after religious rituals had been conducted at the shrine of the Buddha.

Singha Sartha Aju is the *Chakandyo* – a diety – of the Newars who was the first to establish trade ties with Tibet. An ancient *vihar* in his name is located at Thamel in Kathmandu which was built by the merchant prince himself. The temple is believed to house an ancient book with script in gold, and during an annual festival on the day following the full moon day of *Falgun* – the eleventh Nepali month which falls around March – the diety is taken in a procession to Asan and Indrachowk. It is a festival which celebrates Singha Sartha Aju's historic return from Tibet.

Redding Lama

In the interim period until Dalai Lama's incarnation was found, Redding Lama was the provisional head responsible for the Lhasa administration. When the young incarnate was found and brought to Lhasa at the age of six, Redding Lama handed over his responsibilities to the young spiritual ruler.

A rumour was thereafter circulated by the *Kotars* – the rich Tibetan aristocrats – that Redding Lama was a communist. Due to this accusation, in 1943 Redding Lama was one day dragged to the Potala Palace. When he was offered tea by his captors, instead of drinking it, he overturned the cup and said, "Tibet will be overturned in the same manner as this cup." The infuriated nobles then tortured and suffocated him to death. They stuffed *khadas* down his throat, and then throttled him to death with another *khada*.

The rich *Kotars* were in a position to keep servants bought for money, some of whom were mis-treated. In later years, when Tibet was taken over by China, there were instances where the former downtrodden slaves mistreated the captured aristocrats, their former employers.

Redding Lama's monastery at Sera was then plundered by the *Kotars* and all valuables were stolen, confiscated and sold in the Lhasa market. These were brocade, precious stones, valuable statues and bales of high quality woollen textile. Other *Kotars* tried to make a profit for themselves from the plundered goods, and tried to buy whatever they wanted for only a tenth of their market value.

Gyan Jyoti and four other Newars merchants were approached separately by the administering Head Lama of Lhasa. "*Puku* – child – how much would you pay for this?" he would be asked.

This happened several times. One day, Gyan Jyoti suggested politely that they could stop wasting time going round from one trader to another, if they would auction the whole lot, and so be finished with it for once and for all. As the Lama had never heard of an auction before, Gyan Jyoti had to explain in detail how it worked, how everything was to be put out on display. That similar material of similar quality be piled together, in different heaps, and all sold to the highest bidder.

A day was fixed and an auction was organised to sell everything. Among the interested buyers coming to the auction were rich Tibetan merchants including Panda Tshang. The very same Panda Tshang whose brother-in-law Jambala accompanied Gyan Jyoti to Lhasa.

Gyan Jyoti also participated in the bidding, he bid until the prices were brought up in level with the market price and then withdrew from bidding against the rich men. To save face, Panda Tshang had to bid higher than everybody else and ended up paying more for the ware than the actual market price.

The Head Lamas were overjoyed to have made more money than they had dreamed of and in so short a period. Gyan Jyoti was shortly after this, invited to the Potala Palace and asked to pick for himself anything he wanted from the goods they had, and then were surprised when he refused to accept anything. It was completely beyond their understanding.

It was after this incident that the Tibetan officials sought his help and advice for everything, including advice for fixing prices for the local market. They liked and respected him for his openness and his honesty, and invited him to most of their meetings. In this manner his relation with the palace was deepened, and he became the unofficial adviser to the Lhasa administrators, a task which greatly honoured him.

Syamukapu Caravan

The head monk of Dhake Gumbha, Lama Chewang Lhendu, often came to Lhasa to buy goods for his monastery He would come to Gyan Jyoti with his shopping list and ask him to quote his prices. Remembering his father's advise, he wrote down cheaper prices for the goods than the usual market rates. The monk then left and checked prices with other shops before coming back to him to place his orders.

The third or fourth instance when Lama Chewang Lhendu came with his shopping list, he asked for no quotation, instead he handed over his shopping list and said, "*Puku,* what you don't have in your shop, buy it from the market and complete my requirement."

Surprised, Gyan Jyoti asked, "Don't you have to compare prices with the other shops?"

"It is not necessary," said the Lama with a smile. Since then he received regular lists for supplies for the Gumbha, even for items he did not deal with.

One day, when Lama Chewang Lhendu was again at the *Syamukapu kothi* with his shopping list, he said to Gyan Jyoti, "*Puku,* why don't you keep your own mules for transporting goods? This will save you a lot of time. It will take only twenty days to get goods delivered to Kalimpong, and another twenty days for the animals to be back in Lhasa."

143

The norm then was four to five months to get goods transported, as traders often had to wait long for an honest muleteer of their choice who had first to complete earlier consignment of other traders, before taking on another task.

Gyan Jyoti protested he did not have the place to keep the animals nor the possibility to graze them. And finally he had no knowledge about keeping mules. "You only have to agree and all will be taken care of," was the unexpected answer.

Gyan Jyoti said he needed to think about it. He was finally persuaded. Thus the *Syamukapu* business started having its own pack animals. Thirty-five mules were bought with the help of Lama Chewang Lhendu, and the animals were taken care of by men provided by the Gumbha. *Syamukapu* was already a well known and respected name to the Tibetans of Lhasa and Kalimpong, and so the *Syamukapu* caravan was also respected by all in and around Lhasa. Along narrow trails other caravans moved out of the way politely everytime the *Syamukapu* caravan passed by.

Mule trains travelling to Tibet were laden with copper and brass household ware, cymbals and other religious items such as silver and bronze butter lamps for monasteries. Other items were rich Indian brocade, manufactured goods from Calcutta, high quality gold, indigo, *bana* – woollen material, kashmera, bales of cotton textile, watches, tobacco, matches, and felt hats.

When the mule trains plodded back to Kalimpong, they carried with them yak tail, yak wool, bars of silver, gold dust, *jhari* – Tibetan block tea imported from China, Tibetan carpets, *thankas* or *paubas* – religious scroll paintings – Chinese carpets, *kwaychee* – Chinese silk, china ware, and semi-precious stones such as jade, and several other miscellaneous goods.

The Tibetans were rich. A paradoxical statement when one looks at pictures of Tibet and its inhabitants in those early years. A good handful of the Tibetans were indeed rich. The numerous Buddhist monasteries scattered around Tibet were rich, they possessed wealth, their alters were elaborately decorated with gold, silver, precious stones, rich brocade, and valuable *thankas*. The richness of the monasteries were incredible, and indescribable for Newars returning from Tibet.

Gold and silver in dust form were popular in Tibet, and they were in high demand. They were turned into a paste and used for religious works, such as painting statues, elaborate alters and *thanka* scrolls.

Gold was to be found in Tibet. There were two areas where gold was collected, panned from the rivers. They were Nyakcher in the north, and Twascher to the south. The gold dust thus collected was in turn melted and formed into rough bars and balls.

The Tibetan peasants were so naive that they went to the Newar traders with their little finds to confirm if what they had was gold. Some Newars taking advantage of these gullible peasants put the little gold pieces into their mouth pretending that there was a taste to gold, or to have to bite into them to prove their genuiness, and slyly retained in their mouth what they did not want to give back.

Once a year *Milise Gyabu* – the Tibetan Gold King, visited Lhasa to donate his gold to the monasteries and to sell the remaining gold to the Tibetans in Lhasa.

Good established Tibetan families who fled to India and Nepal from the Chinese invasion were said to be later in a position to re-establish themselves in their adopted countries due to the family treasures they were successful in taking out of Tibet.

Departure from Lhasa

At the completion of more than two years in Lhasa, it was time for Gyan Jyoti to return to Kalimpong. The day set for departure was 19th March 1945. Lama Chewang Lhendu was sad to learn that Gyan Jyoti, whom he had grown very fond of, was planning to leave Lhasa. He offered Gyan Jyoti a servant to accompany him on his journey back to Kalimpong.

The servant Pema, turned out to be a big, strong Tibetan and a man of few words. A man who knew his way around the narrow trails and passes of Tibet, he was also very reliable and proved to be an invaluable guide throughout the journey. Pema followed Lama Chewang Lhendu's instructions to the letter, and took personal care of Gyan Jyoti throughout the journey.

On the long journey back to Kalimpong, Gyan Jyoti remembered his one day stay with a Kotar family at Gyantse and laughed about it even after years. Throughout his years in Lhasa, he had remained a vegetarian and so ate a lot of potatoes which to the Tibetans was thought to be very shameful as it was a poor man's meal. With the help of his many *banjas* it had always been possible to eat his potatoes without the knowledge of the Tibetans.

Due to the cold weather, a large bowl with glowing coal was placed for the guests in the room. As soon as the Tibetans had left and they were left to themselves in the room, Barje Bahadur, Gyan Jyoti's *banja* and also his cook, placed some potatoes in the warm ashes to bake them for his *Sahu*. Everytime the *Kotar's* servant came back to the room, he tried to take away the bowl with glowing ashes to add more coal. The horrified Barje Bahadur loudly protested that it was still good enough and did all he could to prevent the *Kotar's* servant from taking the bowl away. With the potatoes still buried in the ashes it was unthinkable that the Tibetans discover the potatoes.

Everytime they were left to themselves again, out came the baked potatoes and Gyan Jyoti was given to eat them. When he felt his *Sahu* had eaten enough for the evening, the *Kotar's* servant was permitted to take away the bowl to put in fresh coal.

Barje Bahadur was a small person, smaller than the usually small Nepalis, and to add to it all, he was incredibly slow in everything he did. And Pema, the Tibetan servant had no patience at all for this slow little Newar. Gyan Jyoti laughed heartily everytime he spoke about the helpless but indignant little Barje Bahadur being picked up by Pema like a sack of potatoes, one hand on his collar and the other hand on his trouser bottom, and thrown atop his mule.

Shortly before Phari, there was very heavy snowfall. The snow was three meters high and to enter the Bhajuratna *kothi* at Phari, they had to enter through the windows on the first floor. This also happened to be the year when Kathmandu experienced its first and last snow fall. At Phari they stayed on for a week due to the weather condition.

At the end of the week, Pema offered to scout the area to look at the possibility of travelling further on in this bad weather. He came back after a few hours to say there was heavy snow only in Phari, but down below there was very little snow. Hence they decided to proceed on their journey.

Once more they had to climb out of the first floor window to continue their onward journey. With Pema as an excellent and cautious guide, they were followed on their journey by other travellers, both Newars and Tibetans all heading in the same direction.

From Yatung they travelled on to Sikkim, and at 15th Mile, they made a halt for the night. Next morning they travelled on to Gangtok, and from there they hired a jeep to take them to Kalimpong.

Kathmandu

On arrival at Kalimpong, Pema was anxious to return to Lhasa immediately. Despite Gyan Jyoti's request to remain in Kalimpong for a few day, Pema wished to go back to his family as soon as possible. Out of gratitude for the special care he had received throughout the journey, Gyan Jyoti gave Pema a large amount of goods for himself and his family members, before allowing him to travel back to Tibet.

When Gyan Jyoti returned from Lhasa, Bhajuratna and his wife were in Nepal, and only Maniharsha was in Kalimpong taking care of business. After a couple of days rest, Gyan Jyoti left for Nepal.

He travelled first to Calcutta by train. For the first time in his life he took the liberty of spoiling himself a little to enjoy the luxury of travelling in a first class carriage. From Calcutta, he travelled on to Raxaul by train, then from Birgunj up to Amlekganj with the narrow gauge railway. From there by truck to Bhimphedi where he made a one night stop, then to Kulekhani on foot, and after another halt the final leg of the journey to Kathmandu.

Throughout the long journey to Kathmandu, Gyan Jyoti had been happily anticipating a warm welcome by proud parents, happy to see their son again after a long absence. Unfortunately, the day he arrived in Kathmandu happened to be a Tuesday, an inauspicious day according to the superstitious Newars, to enter ones house after a long journey.

Despite protests from neighbours and relatives, the very orthodox and conservative Bhajuratna refused to either look at his son or to allow the son who had been away from home for two years, to enter the house.

A disappointed and sad Gyan Jyoti, loaded with money and presents which he had been looking forward to offering to his parents, now had to spend his first night alone in Kathmandu at *Bhansachhen* – the tax house – at Kel Tole, not far from his parent's home.

Early next morning, only after receiving a welcome *puja* and *saga(n)* from his mother at the doorway to the family house, was he finally allowed to enter home to pay his respects to his parents. This was a necessary ceremony to keep away the evil spirits that may have accompanied a traveller from his long journey to far away strange places.

Bhajuratna was very proud of his younger son's Lhasa success. With the large profit his son was able to bring back with him to Kathmandu, he openly showed his appreciation for his younger son, for one and all to notice.

Gyan Jyoti was only twenty four years old when he returned from his successful trip to Lhasa. This was believed to be the turning point where Bhajuratna's sons over the years slowly grew apart from one another, ultimately leading to a tragic family partition some years after the death of Bhajuratna in 1956.

Lhasa Again

Gyan Jyoti undertook his second journey to Lhasa in 1947. This time it was to accompany his younger brother Dev Jyoti, who was to take up the family trade. They were accompanied by Darbay Krishna Kansakar. In Lhasa, he took his younger brother around and introduced him to the job he was in the near future to handle on his own.

After one year of working together, Gyan Jyoti left for Kalimpong, where he returned to take up responsibility for the family business, leaving Dev Jyoti behind as *thakali* of the Syamukapu Lhasa *kothi*.

Dev Jyoti worked in Lhasa for two successful years before returning to Kalimpong, and then like his brother before him, he travelled on to Kathmandu to pay his respects to his parents.

When Gyan Jyoti was in Tibet for the second time from 1947 to 1948, the Lhasa government planned to send a goodwill mission to America, but before this could be undertaken, money had to be deposited as security by the Tibetans in India.

The Tibetan officials looked upon Gyan Jyoti as an honourable businessman, and they liked and trusted him. They finally came to a decision to let him handle the security money on their behalf. With Gyan Jyoti as guarantor, ten lakhs or one million Indian rupees was deposited without any claim of interest by the Tibetan government, at the Bhajuratna office in Calcutta.

Gyan Jyoti was requested to accompany the trade delegation to America as interpreter. He declined. When they approached him again with the same request, hoping he had changed his mind, he declined with the excuse that he was not very good in speaking English. He advised them to take Kuldharma Tuladhar instead, who had a Masters Degree in English and could speak fluent English.

In 1948 Kuldharma Tuladhar accompanied the Tibetan Trade Delegation to the United States as an interpreter.

Business in Wool

Goods entering Kalimpong from Tibet were as already mentioned earlier, Tibetan carpets, Chinese silk carpets, silk from China, *paubha*, *kastu*, jade, *jhari* – Tibetan block tea (from China), yak tail, and wool.

The wool from Tibet was sold to Tibetan merchants living in Kalimpong and also to the Indian traders. It was cleaned and carded in one of the many wool *godowns* of Kalimpong and later re-exported via Calcutta to England and America. The Jyoti Brothers company established by Maniharsha on 15th August 1947 in Calcutta, was given the job of clearing and forwarding goods for merchants of Kathmandu, Lhasa, Calcutta and Kalimpong from the port of Calcutta. From Kalimpong it was wool for Tibetan merchants like Panda Tshang, Sandu Tshang and Reden Tshang.

With the knowledge gained over the months from the wool trade passing through Kalimpong, Gyan Jyoti decided to join in the wool business too. 18th March 1950 he rented a *godown* – a warehouse – in Kalimpong, from a *Marwari* called Samjimall for the monthly rent of ninety rupees.

Tibetan wool traders had their fixed buyers in Kalimpong, however as they knew Gyan Jyoti well from his Lhasa years, they tried to get him to buy some of their wool too. The simple Tibetan wool traders were often cheated by the Indians by manipulating the weighing scales, but nevertheless the

Indians offered good money for their wool, and so they continued selling their wool to the Indians too.

The price Gyan Jyoti offered the Tibetan traders was less, but they still insisted on selling him a portion of their wool. By and by, the simple traders realized that they earned more money selling a few bales to Gyan Jyoti, than what they received from the Indian traders. Gyan Jyoti's honesty in the long run earned him more favours from the Tibetan traders as they later showed a greater preference in dealing with him.

For certain undisclosed reasons, around this period, Jikhachen Gumbha of Tibet had to sell their complete stock of wool. A huge amount worth eight to ten lakhs of Indian rupees. There were long discussions among the concerned Tibetans as to whom to sell it all to. Finally they decided to sell the wool to Gyan Jyoti. His warehouse was small but he was finally persuaded to buy their wool.

As he was walking home in the evening, Panda Tshang, Kalimpong's rich Tibetan merchant happened to drive past in his car. He stopped the car and beckoned to Gyan Jyoti.

"You have taken a very bold step by agreeing to buy so much wool," said the Tibetan.

"I offered a lower price than all the other merchants for the wool, but they still insisted on selling it to me," was the reply.

"Your warehouse is very small, you must buy my warehouse so you have enough place to store all the wool that will be arriving soon."

Gyan Jyoti was alarmed at the suggestion as he did not have the money to invest in a warehouse as well, and frankly said he did not have the money for it.

"My warehouse has also a pressing machine for the wool which will save you the trouble of going to other ware houses. You can pay me in instalment as and when it is convenient for you. Come to my office tomorrow morning at 10 o'clock, and we can discuss this in detail." Saying this, he drove away.

6th April 1953 a deal was made between Panda Tshang and Gyan Jyoti for the wool *godown,* for the sum of sixty thousand rupees, to be paid in instalment. In this manner, Gyan Jyoti became the only Newar to become the owner of one of Kalimpong's largest wool *godown,* and the only Newar also who did business in wool.

He immediately released Samjeelal's small warehouse, and as the months went by, in the warehouse he was now the owner of, he started investing in more money for other facilities, such as an office in the upper floor including an office typewriter and a telephone.

The large open field beside the *godown,* which extended almost up to the top of the hill, was used for the mules on their arrival from Tibet. A long wooden shed at one end of the premises was used to house the Tibetans, and the muleteers. Those were blossoming days for Kalimpong when almost every village woman was employed in one of Kalimpong's wool *godowns.*

The shed beside the *godown* got burnt in the night of 10th November 1967.

Kalimpong Dharmodaya Vihar

At Saranath, under the chairmanship of Ven. Bhadanta Ananda Kaushalyayan, the famous Bhikkhu and one of the most learned scholars of Buddhism in India, a decision was made to establish a committee for maintaining the Dharmodaya Vihar of Kalimpong and to continue Buddhist activities in the town. This was due to the fact that many Buddhist monks were visiting Kalimpong. It was unanimously determined in 1952 to name this committee the Kalimpong Dharmodaya Sabha.

In 1953 the foundation stone for the construction of a stupa in the style of Swoyambhu of Nepal was laid by Ven. Ananda Kaushalyan within the premises of the Kalimpong Vihar, directly above Elza Villa. On its completion the marble statue of Buddha donated by the Buddhists of Burma, was installed.

It was also in 1953 that under the inspiration, guidance and encouragement of Ven. Bhadanta Ananda Kausalyayan, and financial assistance from Gyan Jyoti, the Sabha successfully established the Dharmodaya Hindi School. The Kalimpong Sub-Divisional Officer and the famous Dr. Roerich, a Russian Buddhist scholar, on many occasion consented to distribute prizes and certificates of merit to the students of the Hindi school.

After the successful establishment of the Hindi school, the association also opened a Night College as during this period there were no colleges in Kalimpong, and students had to travel to Darjeeling and other distant places for their higher education. The Night college opened with a limited number of subjects and students, and a separate section for *Pali* was provided. The college functioned successfully for some years but gradually had to be discontinued due to lack of students, when the Indian Government seeing the need, established a college in Kalimpong.

Due to the existence of the Dharmodaya Vihar, Kalimpong was over the years visited regularly by several learned Bhikkhus and Buddhist scholars.

Bhikkhu Sangharakkita, a brilliant Buddhist scholar, stayed at the Kalimpong Vihar for fourteen years. During his years in Kalimpong, the monthly Buddhist magazine "Stepping Stones" came into publication in English, and the Young Men's Buddhist Association (YMBA) was also established. Regular articles were contributed to the "Stepping Stones" by Dr. George Roerich, Prince Peter of Greece and Denmark, Ian David Macdonald, Dr. Wojkowitz, among some of the many well known names around Kalimpong. Rev. Sangharakkita was President of the publication, Dr. Roerich was its Adviser, and Gyan Jyoti the Treasurer.

Regular religious lectures and discourses were organized at the Vihar. There were weekly educational film shows presented by the YMBA, which attracted large audiences. The projector and other equipment, including the regular supply of films were contributed by the United States Information Service.

The teachings of the Buddha Dhamma given by Bhikkhu Sangharakkita were very inspiring and stimulating, so that many came to listen to him. He became so well known that he was also invited by the Maharaja of Sikkim to give such discourses in Sikkim as well.

It was a sad day for Kalimpong when Bhikkhu Sangharakkita after living for many years at the Dharmodaya Vihar left to continue his work in Calcutta.

Bhikkhu Ananda Kausalyayan also stayed at the Kalimpong Vihar for several years and guided the Dharmodaya Sabha in its various religious activities. When trade with Tibet declined due to political disturbances on the other side of the border, and the closure of the India Tibet border, many Lhasa Newars gave up their business and properties in Kalimpong and returned to Kathmandu. This therefore resulted in the Vihar losing its main financial support, as it was mainly supported by the Lhasa Newars.

In 1963, Kalimpong Dharmodaya Sabha became a member of the World Fellowship of Buddhists (WFB), as a result of the efforts of Bhikkhu Mahanam Mahasthabir. Since then, Gyan Jyoti as the President along with other members of the Sabha, participated regularly in several international WFB conferences, in Japan, Hong Kong, Korea, Thailand and Taiwan.

The Dharmodaya Nursery School of Kalimpong was established in 1984, in the premises of the Vihar. Various members of the Sabha supported and financed the school during its early years. Punya Bahadur Shakya and Prem Kazi Shakya deserve to be particularly commended on their determination and perseverance for the success of the school. Gyan Jyoti supported it with financial assistance and encouragement during the initial trying period, when funds were sorely required to keep the school running, and for the monthly salary of the teachers.

In the late eighties there was a campaign by the local Indian municipality to take over all vacant land plots in and around Kalimpong, including the empty wool godown and its land at Topkhana. To prevent this action, on 9th June 1990 Gyan Jyoti donated the wool godown and its property to the Kalimpong Dharmodaya Sabha. The property was then sold by Dharmodaya Sabha to the Darjeeling Gorkha Hill Council on 10th August 1990 and the in-coming money was used to fund the expansion of the Dharmodaya Nursery School.

Today, the old wool godown has been converted into Sahid Park, and every year on 27th July, Sahid Diwas, or Martyrs Memorial Day is celebrated here.

The 2500th Buddha Jayanti

For all the Buddhists of the world the full moon day of Baishak, is a day of celebration and prayers, as it is the day Lord Buddha was born, received enlightenment and died. 1956 was an even more special year, as it marked 2500 years of this special occasion. To commemorate the event, the Mahabodhi Society of India, a large Buddhist organisation with branches all over India, invited the Dalai Lama to join them in their celebration.

The Dharmodaya Sabha also organized one of the most elaborate Buddhist function in Kalimpong. Gyan Jyoti took on the responsibility of getting the support of the King of Bhutan. He also approached Shakapa the Tibetan Finance Minister for support from Tibet. The Theravada monks of Kalimpong got together to draw up their own program for the day. What finally resulted was the culmination of the biggest and most colourful event ever organized in Kalimpong, which was the talk of the town for years after.

Days ahead, the local people prepared colourful paper flags to decoratively line the streets of Kalimpong, and to hang them around the Buddhist monasteries. Strings of yarn were tied up between posts, and then thin sheets of paper in various bright colour were cut into even triangles and pasted on the extended yarn with glue, then left to dry. Children were ready helpers for such tasks, and cheerfully competed with one another to prepare the longest streamers.

The Karmapa arrived in Kalimpong with some of his monks, who were sent to participate in the procession. The King of Bhutan gave his permission to allow some important and valuable statues to be used during the procession. The long colourful procession included high Lamas from both Tibet, Bhutan and Sikkim, Lamas with their religious drums and horns, followed by Tibetan, Sikkimese and Bhutanese lay people in their full festive clothes, carrying banners and Buddhist flags.

The Theravada monks of Kalimpong also joined the Lamas in the long procession. Finally, different ethnic groups of Kalimpong followed, and all this ended at the *mela* ground, where prayers were held, and the inevitable speeches given. The procession of Lamas then went on to the Dharmodaya Vihar to offer prayers at Buddha's shrine.

For the rest of the day, the Dharmodaya Vihar had organized an all day program with special prayer services, religious discussions, refreshments, and a Buddhist exhibition, to which people thronged through out the day.

Special Occasions

The late King Mahendra of Nepal while still a crown prince visited Darjeeling and Kalimpong in 1952, to inspect schools for his sons. The final choice for the royal children was Saint Joseph's College North Point, in Darjeeling, an all boys school established by the Jesuits.

Gyan Jyoti heard about this and so drove to Darjeeling to extend an invitation to the crown prince to visit Kalimpong, on behalf of all the Newars living there. The request was readily accepted. Prince Mahendra's private secretary Lok Darshan Bajracharya suggested that the community in Kalimpong organize a function where the future king could be welcomed, which would be better than taking him on a sight seeing tour.

A welcome function for the future king was held at the Dharmodaya Vihar, where the Newars had the opportunity of informing him about their businesses in Lhasa and Kalimpong. Lunch in honour of the crown prince was hosted at the Bhutan House by the King of Bhutan, who took the occasion to be in Kalimpong for the royal visitor of Nepal. It must be remembered here that Kalimpong is only a three hours car journey from Bhutan, and so it was no difficulty for the royal family to be travelling frequently to Kalimpong. In the afternoon the royal visitor was invited to dinner by Prince Peter of Greece, who was then living in Kalimpong.

At the end of the functions in Kalimpong, Gyan Jyoti then drove the royal visitor back to Darjeeling, where other receptions awaited the royal guest from Nepal.

Prince Peter of Greece was an anthropologist who had made Kalimpong his home. However, around 1959 when Tibetans were fleeing to India, Sikkim, Bhutan and Nepal from the Chinese occupation in Tibet, foreigners were suspected by the Indian government. Foreigners, such as some British journalists, including Prince Peter were asked to leave Kalimpong on grounds of their sympathy with Tibet.

His Holiness the Dalai Lama visited Kalimpong the first time in 1957. The Dalai Lama had been to Delhi to meet with Prime Minister Nehru to discuss the Chinese occupation and deteriorating conditions in Tibet. 17th January 1957, he stopped over in Calcutta, where Gyan Jyoti who was in Calcutta shortly after his father's death, met him. A couple of months later the Dalai Lama visited Kalimpong. While in Kalimpong the Dalai Lama stayed at Bhutan House, and Gyan Jyoti was later among the guests waiting there to welcome him, and many Tibetans living in Kalimpong flocked to see their religious leader.

It was also during this visit that a special reception was held in the Dalai Lama's honour at Dr. Graham's Homes. One day, as Gyan Jyoti was going to Bhutan House to pay his respects to the Dalai Lama, he met some Lhasa Newars standing outside the gates of Bhutan House. They proposed that an arrangement be made to invite the Dalai Lama to the Dharmodaya Vihar, so all the Buddhist Newars would have the opportunity to pay their respect too. The request was extended and the Dalai Lama despite his busy schedule agreed to visit the Vihar and meet the Newars for a few minutes.

Preparations were hurriedly made to receive the Dalai Lama. A welcome gate in brocade was erected at the entrance to the Dharmodaya Vihar at the cost of fifty thousand rupees, an elaborate expensive gate for a short, but special event. After a *puja* was performed and the people present were blessed, the Dalai Lama was surprised and happy to be able to speak in Tibetan to the Newars present, and to learn that many of the men had lived and worked in Lhasa for some years. And so an intended short visit of fifteen minutes was extended to over thirty minutes.

In 1957 when Prime Minister Jawaharlal Nehru visited Darjeeling, selected businessmen from Darjeeling, Kalimpong and Siliguri were given invitations to meet him on his arrival at the Bagdogra airport. Gyan Jyoti was selected from Kalimpong and was given the opportunity of being introduced to Mr. Nehru.

During the 1960s, Dudjom Rinpoche of the Nyingmapa school of Tibetan Buddhism had his residence in Kalimpong. At the start of 1970 he lived partly in Kathmandu, where he had bought a house in Thamel, a few blocks away from Gyan Jyoti's house. He moved to a monastery donated to him in France in the mid 1970s and died there 17th January 1987. Two years later Dudjom Rinpoche's body was flown back to Kathmandu, where he was entombed in a monastery in Boudhanath. For this occasion, day long ceremonies were performed, which was attended by hundreds of devotees, including many of his followers from Europe and America.

The Sixteenth Karmapa

His Holiness the Sixteenth Karmapa was born 1924 in Denkhok, in the Derge province of Eastern Tibet, as Rangjung Rigpa'i Dorje. The Karmapa monastery at Tsurpu, the traditional seat of the Karmapa, was established in the twelfth century. He is the spiritual leader of one of the four major schools of Tibetan Buddhism, ranking behind the Dalai Lama and the Panchen Lama in spiritual hierarchy.

7th October 1950, Chamdo the capital of Eastern Tibet was attacked and occupied by the Chinese army. 9th September 1951, the Chinese troops marched into Lhasa. Over the years, several efforts made by the Dalai Lama with the Chinese government to come to a peaceful solution failed. Realizing that the situation in Tibet would not improve, the Karmapa after informing the Dalai Lama left his Tsurpu Monastery, and fled from Tibet in early 1959 followed by one hundred and sixty monks, nuns and lay people, and arrived in Bhutan.

He was later joined by other Tulkus already in Bhutan, who had also fled from Tibet. Chogyal Tashi Namgyal, the King of Sikkim, offered the Karmapa and his monks the possibility to settle in Sikkim, and so Rumtek Monastery was selected, which is believed to have been built by a King of Sikkim under the guidance of the 9th Karmapa. Rumtek 1547m. high, is located 24 km. south-east from Gangtok, a forty-five minute car drive away. But as the crow flies only 6 km. away.

In the spring of 1959, the Dalai Lama also escaped from Tibet and took political refuge in India, where he settled down at Dharamsala in North India, with his monks and followers.

The Karmapa appealed to merchants of Gangtok and Kalimpong for assistance in supporting the monks who had followed him out of Tibet. Gyan Jyoti offered to take care of four monks, one of them was Gendun Rinpoche. The four monks then lived in his house at the 11th Mile in Kalimpong for the next twelve years.

Until the new monastery at Rumtek was completed, the Karmapa lived in the old Rumtek monastery. The construction of the new monastery started in 1962 and it was finally inaugurated in 1966.

In 1961, the Karmapa charitable Trust was founded by the Sixteenth Karmapa. It was only after the Karmapa's death in 1981 that all the seven lay trustee members including Gyan Jyoti came to hear of its existence for the first time. Later Shamar Rinpoche, Kongtrul Rinpoche and Situ Rinpoche became members of the Trust as successors to three initial lay trustees. The function of the Trustees ended in May 2004, with the coming of age of the Seventeenth Karmapa.

From the first contact in 1947, Gyan Jyoti had a very deep and special relationship with the Sixteenth Karmapa. The Karmapa always sent him a telegram before his departure for Kalimpong, Calcutta or Kathmandu, and no matter where he was, Gyan Jyoti always made the effort to be there with the Karmapa during these visits.

The Karmapa was several times in Kalimpong and always stayed at the Bhajuratna Kothi at 11th Mile, arriving with his entourage of monks and servants. Hundreds of devotional Tibetans flocked to the 11th Mile all day to pay their homage, and the Black Hat ceremony was performed during some of these visits. The Bhutan Royal family often came to meet the Karmapa and also to attend the ceremonies. On several occasion Shamar Rinpoche and his brother Jigmila accompanied the Karmapa on these frequent trips to Kalimpong.

While Gyan Jyoti lived in Kalimpong, he often took the opportunity of travelling to Rumtek either alone or with his family, to pay his respects to Karmapa. It was very seldom, that he came away from these visits without receiving a present of some kind or other from the Karmapa. A pen, a camera, framed pictures, photos, and whatever else happened to be at hand, besides the frequent gifts of consecrated mani pills and powdered incense. No other visitors would be allowed into the room, when Gyan Jyoti was with the Karmapa.

The first time that Gyan Jyoti travelled to Rumtek with his family was to accompany the Karmapa's niece Chimey to be with her mother in Rumtek, over her three months school winter holidays.

The journey to Rumtek with the six year old Chimey and the family was an adventure. There was then no proper motor way connecting Gangtok to Rumtek. From a certain starting point in Gangtok, they travelled on horseback to Rumtek, with Tibetan guides on foot guiding the horse of each child, so they would not fall off when going up or down the steep mountain trails. In comparison to the shorter trail Gyan Jyoti normally took on his visits to Rumtek, they were guided through a longer but much easier route to Rumtek. It was not an easy journey, as the tracks were narrow and steep sometimes. Despite the hair raising journey, it was an exciting experience for Gyan Jyoti's children and his wife who were riding horses for the first time as a means of travel. A totally different experience from the pony rounds in Darjeeling around the Chowrasta area.

Chimey spent parts of her school holidays with Gyan Jyoti's family over the two year period when she went to St. Joseph's Convent, a missionary boarding school in Kalimpong, with his two daughters. After two years she was sent to America to continue her schooling. Many years later, the family learned through His Holiness the Karmapa that Chimey had completed her education and was back in Sikkim. A happy reunion took place when the family met her again in Gangtok. A young attractive woman finally back in Sikkim, she had over the long years in the States forgotten the Nepali and Tibetan languages, but had not lost her Asian charm. Today, she lives in Kathmandu.

For some years, Gyan Jyoti went through a difficult period after the partition with his brothers in 1964. During this period, the Karmapa tried to uplift his spirit and often gave his special blessings. He prophesied that Gyan Jyoti's troubles would soon be over, and that happy successful years were ahead of him.

In 1967 Raja Dorjee, the King of Bhutan died, so the Karmapa was invited to Bhutan to perform the religious last ceremonies. Gyan Jyoti received an invitation to participate in the ceremonies by the government of Bhutan, which he readily accepted. For almost a week, as a State Guest of Bhutan, he lived at the Bhutan Royal Palace, and was given a room next to the Karmapa. And every day, he joined the Karmapa to take meals together with the new King of Bhutan.

For Gyan Jyoti all this was an unforgettable experience and a great honour.

Through the Karmapa, Gyan Jyoti and the family got to know Mrs. Bedi.

An Englishwoman, Mrs. Bedi had previously been a Theravada nun, but she had left the order to marry an Indian and moved with him to India. They had three children, one of them Kabir Bedi grew to become a famous Indian actor.

When Tibetan refugees started pouring into India, Mrs. Bedi got herself involved. In 1961 she opened a school in her house in Delhi for Tibetan *Tulkus* – reincarnate lamas – where they could study Buddhist philosophy and learn the English language. She personally helped to get them all sponsors through her contacts in Europe. The school was later moved to Dalhousie in 1963, a hillstation in Northern India.

Mrs. Bedi left her husband to become a follower of the Karmapa and was ordained a nun by the Karmapa. It was during one of his visits to Rumtek that Gyan Jyoti was introduced to Mrs. Bedi by the Karmapa, and since then she visited Kalimpong a few times, and stayed at Gyan Jyoti's house. Once Mrs. Bedi was at the 11th Mile house again when Gyan Jyoti's children were home for the school holidays. She suggested that they become pen friends with her children, but the idea was never taken up seriously.

Although ordained as Sister Kechong Palmo, she was always referred to as Mrs. Bedi by everybody, including the Karmapa, when talking about her. She died in May 1977.

The Karmapa was several times in Kathmandu in the 1970s and stayed at the Tibetan Gumbha next to the Swoyambhu Stupa. In later years, he stayed at his new Gumbha behind the Boudhanath stupa. The first time His

Holiness visited Gyan Jyoti's newly completed house in Thamel, he blessed the house and all the rooms. Starting from the top he slowly walked down, all the while murmuring a prayer and throwing a few corns of rice in each direction.

During a later visit, when the new building with the office was complete, at Gyan Jyoti's request, His Holiness blessed the new building and the office. He took a special delight sitting on Gyan Jyoti's office chair and swivelling himself around like a child.

Gyan Jyoti's last meeting with the Karmapa was in 1981 in Rumtek. The Karmapa had opened Buddhist centres in Europe and the United States, and was often travelling to one of these new centres. Gyan Jyoti came to learn that the Karmapa was in Rumtek again, but would be leaving for America soon.

Plans were quickly made to meet His Holiness before he left Rumtek. On this last visit, Gyan Jyoti was accompanied by his wife and elder daughter. The Karmapa was suffering from cancer and had lost a lot of weight. His travel to America within the next few weeks was for another cancer treatment.

The Karmapa was very fond of animals, especially dogs and birds. He always had one or two small dogs sitting beside him, or running around the room, sniffing inquisitively at the many visitors, and a bird or two in a cage in the room.

A large group of Sikkimese were getting ready to leave when Gyan Jyoti arrived at the Rumtek monastery with his family. Once the room was empty, and *khadas* had been offered to the Karmapa, he made a sign that Gyan Jyoti and his family take a seat closer to him. They were hardly seated when Tibetan butter tea was served by a lama hovering in the background. It always tasted nice at the monastery. The

Karmapa was interested in knowing the latest about each member of the family, about the grand children, and about his business. He laughed a lot as he always did, as he tried a little of his Nepali on Gyan Jyoti's wife. He then talked long in Tibetan about his travels to Europe and America, and the different centres, with Gyan Jyoti intentively listening to him.

The family were asked to remain for lunch which was then served in the same room. It was as if the Karmapa knew this was his last meeting with the family. After lunch was over, he asked them if they would like to join him to see his birds. Together they all followed His Holiness out of the monastery and walked to the garden which was part of a large aviary. There were birds of different sizes and colour, exotic birds, sitting on branches, strutting around, and although they did not feel disturbed by the visitors, they kept at a safe distance.

At one end of the aviary was a large double storied building which was also visited, where still more birds were flying freely around the rooms. The Karmapa looked very happy to be among the birds, and laughed to see the amazed looks of his three guests. Gyan Jyoti's daughter finally picked up the courage to ask the Karmapa if she could take a photo of him and her father together. It is unfortunate that during this unforgettable day together, the opportunity was not used to take as many photos as possible of the Karmapa among his birds.

Back in the monastery, the Karmapa again suggested to Gyan Jyoti that he visit France with his family to meet Gendun Rinpoche, and if he needed help, Jigmela was also there in France. As always, the invitation was also extended to use the opportunity to visit the Karmapa centres in America, and to stay at the centres whenever he wished. His parting gift to the family as they got ready to leave was a set of four framed sketches of birds.

A few months later, on 5th November 1981, the sad news went around the world that His Holiness the Karmapa had passed away at a hospital in Chicago.

9th November his body was flown back to Sikkim, and the funeral ceremony was held at Rumtek monastery on 20th December 1981. Gyan Jyoti attended the ceremony with his wife and family members, including his grand children.

Happy Days in Kalimpong

Kalimpong was home for Gyan Jyoti and his growing family. Beside his daily business, he turned to other interests during his spare time. His interest turned to flowers. Two local gardeners were employed, a green house was built, and the lawn around the 11th Mile house was soon turned into a colourful garden with flowers blossoming all the year round.

Bees were introduced to pollinate and improve the quality of the flowers, and several bee hives were installed around the whole complex. This resulted in a bee keeper having to come regularly to check all the bee hives. With dozens of bee hives around the garden, a small centrifuge was brought into the house to extract honey. Scores of orange trees had been planted around the complex, when the oranges were ripe, a local trader came along with his truck and helpers, and trucked away the oranges, leaving some trees untouched for family consumption.

The family was never short of fruits throughout the year. There were leeche and jackfruit trees. Bananas, plums, peaches and guavas grew in abundance. With a beautiful garden, and the constant fragrance of blossoms in the air, the place resembled a little paradise.

Gyan Jyoti started participating every year in the Annual Kalimpong Flower Show. He won several awards and certificates for individual flowers exhibited at the Town Hall, which in later years he never failed to proudly show to all his house guests. He also participated in the small Garden competition, and for three consecutive years, 1964, 1965 and 1966 he won the first prize for Kalimpong's Small Garden competition, until the organizers had to request him to refrain from participating the following year, to give other participants the opportunity of winning too. School children came in groups to enjoy the garden. One regular visitor was Joe Macdonald with the school children of Dr. Graham's Homes.

With more than half a dozen special breed cows at the farm, a *gobargas* plant – biogas – was installed not far from the green house, and the gas used for cooking for some years. The excess milk produced from the cows was sold in the local market, and there was a non stop supply of home made butter and yoghurt. The initiator of this project was Parasmani Pradhan, a well known name in the literary circle of Kalimpong. With the help of an instruction book in his possession and a Gyan Jyoti willing to experiment, the two men got together to build the *gobargas* plant, which became the focus of interest in Kalimpong.

On the first floor of the house was the *deyo kotha* – prayer room – which was used all day and every day by Gendun Rinpoche and the other three monks. It was also the prayer room used by the Karmapa on his visits to Kalimpong. The monks prayed from morning to evening everyday, as they did in a monastery, and between their breaks they walked around the garden. When the children came home for their school holidays, the first thing they had to do was go into the prayer room to greet the four monks. And before returning to school, there was a final visit to the *deyo kotha* to light incense sticks and butter lamps at the alter, and to say goodbye to the four monks.

Most of the *banjas* employed whether in Calcutta, Lhasa or Kalimpong were from and around the Kathmandu Valley. The people employed at the Bhajuratna *kothi* were of different nature and temperament, and it was seldom but not unusual that sometimes friction arose between some of them, often due to language problem.

At times it could turn hilarious. A locally employed gardener disliked being served food prepared the previous day. While being served his lunch by a new Newar cook, the fussy gardener demanded: "Y*o kailay ko achar!*" Prompt came the answer, "*Bholi ko!*" The cook not yet sure of his Nepali had confused his Nepali words for yesterday and tomorrow. The surprised gardener without another comment quietly ate the *achar* for tomorrow, amid smothered guffaws from the other servants. Or for instance, other misunderstandings arising from a Newar confusing his word *talay* – upstairs, with the Nepali word *talaa* for downstairs.

Many *Jyapus* – Newar farmers of the Kathmandu Valley – spent their free time in the evenings learning to read and write, and sharing their newly acquired knowledge with the new comers.

Kalimpong wore a festive air during *Sunti* – the Tihar festival of lights. Many business houses decorated the entrance to their buildings with an archway erected with large leafy banana plants, and the windows and doorways with garlands of marigold flowers. Indian film songs played on gramophones at full blast, echoed the air from morning to evening, and as soon as it got dark, children went in groups from house to house singing and collecting money, a tradition which is carried on in Nepal too.

Fire crackers exploded at unexpected corners and spectacular fire works lit up the dark evening sky. Lights when switched on in the evening signalled the start of open house at all offices and shops. Laxmi, the goddess of wealth was worshipped in the evening, by one and all.

Friends and acquaintances strolled through town in groups, walking into different shops and offices, to collect free nuts, and sweets and *pan* – beetle leaf – and to see which *Sahu* had decorated his shop the nicest. This was the period when all the carpets were collected from the 11th Mile *kothi*, to carpet the normally bare floored office rooms of the 10th Mile building.

A favourite pastime at the Bhajuratna *kothi* during *Sunti* – the Newar New Year – was playing cards with their *Sahu* against small money late into the night. It was the only period when gambling was officially permitted. The servants always lost, but never realized that Gyan Jyoti often managed to cheat them at the card games.

Besides being the President of the Kalimpong Dharmodaya Sabha for several years, Gyan Jyoti was also elected a committee member of the SUMI School Board, his old school, a post which he held for a couple of years. During this period, he donated a large pure silver cup to the school, to be used as a rotating trophy for school tournaments. It was called the Bhajuratna Cup.

Mining in India

In 1958 business expanded to mining in South India, starting with a mine leased at Jhalandari near Bhilai, where iron ore and manganese were extracted in open air mines. Approximately four thousand people were employed at the mine.

Bhilai lies in central India, in the State of Madhya Pradesh, over two hundred kilometers from the city of Nagpur. An extremely hot and dry area, it used to be an area infested by scorpions, snakes and tigers. Over the years, Gyan Jyoti and Laxmi Prabha spent many months in this village near Bhilai, which until the early 1960s was only a small settlement. His children also spent several weeks there over their three month school winter holidays.

A dry dusty area, there were little rock like ant hills every where which the children were told to avoid. The toilets were located some distance outside the living quarters, which was a problem in the dark. Going to the toilet before bed-time was a hair raising experience. Walking in a file behind each other, with only a torch to light the way, they had to make sure they did not accidentally step onto a scorpion. Or to move cautiously, swinging the torch rays left and right, so if there was a snake nearby, it had time to slither away.

Fortunately for the family, there were no encounters with tigers, but the villagers often brought tales of having spotted a tiger somewhere. Mining plots were given numbers, with

Number 10 mine being located the furthest away. It was here at this location that the miners had the most excitement, as it was here that a tiger was often spotted. With loud shouts and beating of tin cans, the prowling animals would be chased away from the vicinity.

Gyan Jyoti was permitted to own a rifle for protection against the tigers, but in all the years the family lived in Bhilai, it was never used at all. The rifle accompanied the family whenever they went on sightseeing tours with the Landrover. When driving through a forested area, the driver would point out to the enraptured children spoors left by animals across the dusty tracks. Trying to spot tiger spoors while driving along these dusty roads were scary but exciting, especially if several spoors could be spotted together, which meant a water hole was not far away.

Once there was a great uproar from the mining field. A leopard had been spotted and was killed by the villagers, as it was on its way to a water hole with its young ones. It was illegal to kill the wild animals, and so for days, the villagers hid the leopard under a truck, until it was safe to sneak it away.

In the house, there was always a supply of bandages, plasters and medicine such as tablets, ointment and iodine for the normal everyday mild health problems. One day Laxmi Prabha tended to a villager with a cut on his arm, with a good dab of iodine. A few days later, wanting to be similarly treated, more villagers working at the mine turned up in front of the house, with mild cuts and wounds, and slowly a line of villagers kept queuing up daily for medical aid.

Around this period, the Russian government built the Bhilai Steel Plant, and the ore required was delivered by the Jyoti Brothers company. In February of 1959 the Bhilai Steel

Plant was inaugurated by the President of India, to which Gyan Jyoti as Director of the mining company was invited.

Attired in his everyday Nepali outfit, a white *kameez sulwar* – shirt and trousers – Gyan Jyoti due to his fluent Hindi was mistaken as an Indian by the Minister for Mines Swaran Singh. A Punjabi himself, he mistook Gyan Jyoti for a fellow Punjabi. Minister Swaran Singh was at first astonished and then pleased to learn that he was addressing a Nepali. He shook hands heartily, and with a friendly arm around him for the next few minutes, exclaimed that he was happy that a Nepali was capable of undertaking such an enterprise. Till then all the Nepali people he had ever come into contact with were much sought after *darwans* – watchmen and guards – or Gorkha soldiers.

After the death of Bhajuratna in 1956, the business he had founded through his hard work continued to expand while at the same time the sons were slowly growing apart. Under the registered name of Jyoti Brothers Maniharsha handled business from Calcutta, Dev Jyoti from Kathmandu, and Gyan Jyoti from Kalimpong. With effect from 4th July 1964, the two brothers separated from Gyan Jyoti, giving him the sole responsibility of Jyoti Brothers, and the business in India. The lease of the Bhilai mine had been terminated shortly before the three brothers legally separated.

Gyan Jyoti took over the head office in Calcutta, and renewed the iron ore mining business in south India. First he leased the Chitradurga Mine in the south Indian state of Karnataka (previously known as Mysore State) which was inaugurated 10th November 1965. Another mine at Chiknayakanhalli, located in the district of Tumkur was also leased and operated by Gyan Jyoti under the name of Jyoti Brothers. Both mines were operated from the regional office of Chitradurga, with Yogya Ratna Tamrakar as site manager for both mines, and two years later an office and an apartment were set up in Bangalore.

The mining business developed well, the plan now was for the family to settle down in Bangalore. Gyan Jyoti's mother died unexpectedly in February 1969, while he and the family were in Kathmandu on a short visit. This upset all his plans for the family. With the traditional death rites stretching over the year, Laxmi Prabha was forced to stay on in Kathmandu to participate in the rites. One thing lead to another, and slowly the thought of settling in Bangalore had to be abandoned.

For Gyan Jyoti's family, Bangalore and the surrounding areas in South India were full of interest. From Bangalore, there were frequent visits to the beaches of Madras including museums, parks, the Tungabhadra dam and other interesting places in the near lying areas. Mysore was a favourite place with its majestic Maharaja's Palace, a fairy tale spectacle. It is especially magnificent during Dasain, the Hindu festival of Dushera, when it is illuminated by no less than 8000 light bulbs.

There used to be an annual event in Mysore, an extravagant display on the tenth of the last day of the Dushera festival. A magnificent procession of mounted guardsmen on horses and richly decorated elephants carrying the Maharaja of Mysore and the royal family, went around in a stately procession.

Gyan Jyoti together with his wife and daughters were witness to this last historical event which took place in 1970. Watching from seats in a dais opposite the royal pavilion, the start of the royal procession could be closely followed. First the Maharaja got on a caparisoned elephant. He was followed by his adolescent son on a similarly caparisoned elephant. As the young Prince bent to get onto the howdah, a murmur of consternation went up through the crowd. The royal turban had slipped from the royal head. A careless act on the part of the young Prince, and a bad omen for the Maharaja of Mysore.

No one in the crowd realized it then, but this was to be the last procession for the Maharaja of Mysore. Some months later, Prime Minister Indira Gandhi brought to end the era of all the Maharajas of India, closing a glorious chapter in the history of India.

The Mysore Palace has since then been turned into a museum, and is open to visitors. All come away in amazement, unable to believe in the richness of the palace, and a way of life only to be dreamed of.

With age catching up, and his desire to settle down with his family in Nepal, he slowly disliked making the frequent long train journey to South India, and gradually left the business in the hands of his efficient manager Mr. Nabi, who took over when Yogya Ratna returned to Calcutta.

Goodbye Kalimpong

With the China India war of 1962, trade with Tibet came to a final stop. Almost all the Lhasa Newars returned to Kathmandu and Kalimpong went back to becoming a quiet sleepy town.

After the family split in 1964, Gyan Jyoti and Laxmi Prabha spent more time in Calcutta, with regular visits to Kalimpong and whenever the children had their school holidays. The four Tibetan monks continued to live at the 11th Mile house with Gyan Jyoti's younger sister Gyan Shova managing the house with servants from Kathmandu. Circa 1972, the monks left Kalimpong to live in a monastery in Bhutan, at the instruction of His Holiness the Karmapa.

After the arranged marriage of Gyan Jyoti's youngest daughter Dharma Shova to Swoyambhu Ratna Tuladhar of Kathmandu, in 1973, Gyan Shova remained in Kathmandu. She continued to live with her brother and his family in Kathmandu until her untimely death in June 1993. The house in Kalimpong was left under the care of a *Jyapu* family especially selected from the Kathmandu Valley.

Gyan Jyoti's grandchild was admitted into St. Joseph's Convent in Kalimpong in 1982, and the other grandchildren followed in the following years. The family members then had to go to Kalimpong twice a year to take the children to school and to pick them up during their school holidays. These opportunities were taken to spend time at the 11th Mile house again, although it was not the same anymore with all its empty rooms and its bare lawns. All the same, the grandchildren grew to love the house.

Gyan Jyoti and his wife decided it was not easy living in Kathmandu and taking care of property in Kalimpong. The house had to be regularly maintained, and the municipality taxes had to be paid. A caretaker was required to live permanently in the house with his family, to take care of the house and extensive land.

There were long discussions in the family, it was finally decided to donate the house to the Karmapa. It was a house that had experienced history over the last fifty years, and with the Karmapa, it would be in good hands. Shamar Rinpoche was informed about the intended plan and an appointment was made to meet in Kalimpong.

17th September 1991, Gyan Jyoti travelled to Kalimpong accompanied by his elder daughter, to hand over the house and the keys to the house to Shamar Rinpoche. Also included were the fourteen hectares of land surrounding it and the steep motorway leading down to the property. It was a sad decision, but it was the best thing that could happen to the family property. It was a house which had witnessed much, and had been a home for Bhajuratna, his children and grandchildren, for many happy years.

The afternoon of 17th September was spent walking around the property with Shamar Rinpoche, and pointing out to him all the land that belonged to the Bhajuratna Kothi. Shamar Rinpoche who was unused to the exertion of going up and down the slopes surrounding the house, was soon out of breath as he tried to keep up with the seventy year old but agile Gyan Jyoti, who showed no signs of exhaustion. Gyan

Jyoti was even able to keep up a conversation with Shamar Rinpoche all the way, until they got back to the house again.

Since the house was donated, Gyan Jyoti and Laxmi Prabha were back in Kalimpong several times, and during every visit they stayed at the 11th Mile house. This time as guests of the Seventeenth Karmapa. The nicest memory of it all for Gyan Jyoti was to see the garden well cared for and in full blossom again, the way it always used to be, and just the way he loved it.

Gendun Rinpoche

Lama Gendun Rinpoche was the meditation master and spiritual director of Dhagpo Kagyu Ling, France. A Meditator of vast accomplishment, he had passed more than thirty years of his life in solitary retreat in Tibet and India. His Holiness Karmapa when presenting him in Europe, in order to guide those wishing to enter the path of inner understanding, said: "In the person of Gendun Rinpoche, I make the gift to you of a pure jewel."

(Dagpo-Kagyu-Ling magazine, 1996)

Gendun Rinpoche escaped from Tibet circa 1959 and went to Rumtek to meet the Karmapa who had himself successfully escaped from Tibet. Shortly after his arrival, the Karmapa appealed to rich merchants of Gangtok and Kalimpong for assistance in supporting the over hundred monks who had followed him out of Tibet. It was around 1960, that Gyan Jyoti offered to take into his house in Kalimpong four monks. Gendun Rinpoche and Lama Pourtse were among the four.

Some months after the four monks had settled down in Kalimpong, Gyan Jyoti took his family on a pilgrim tour around India. The group included his wife and three children, his unmarried younger sister Gyan Shova, and his mother-in-law. They were accompanied by the four Tibetan monks and a Tibetan servant named Kapta. The pilgrimage ended with a visit to the World Exhibition which was hosted in New Delhi.

The four monks lived at the Bhajuratna Kothi in Kalimpong for the next twelve years until circa 1972, when at the instruction of His Holiness the Karmapa, they left for a monastery in Bhutan. Gendun Rinpoche and Lama Sonam Pourtse were sent to France in 1975 to help support Karmapa's newly established Kagyu Centre.

In 1994, Gyan Jyoti participated in a World Buddhist Conference in Bangkok. Some days later, while visiting a departmental store in Bangkok, he came across a Chinese palm reader, and like all Asians, could not resist having his palm read.

"Ooh! Yes Sir, you very very rich man Sir." Still looking closely at his palm, the man said, "You travel to end of Europe Sir. Yes Sir, you too much rich Sir! And you very, very strong. Very strong man Sir, you live until 85 years."

The man of course got a good tip for saying such nice things to his customer. The palm reader also predicted that his elder daughter would get married soon.

In the spring of 1995, Deb Shova got married to Hans Hilker of Germany and went to live in Germany. In the summer of 1996, Gyan Jyoti finally accepted their invitation to visit them in Germany, and to use the opportunity to see a bit of Europe. This was his first travel to Europe. It was exactly as predicted by the Chinese palm reader.

His first wish on arrival, was to visit Keukenhoef in Holland. It is a paradise for flower lovers, and he was the best proof that the fame of Keukenhoef was limited not only to the Europeans. It was the beginning of May, when Tulips of every shade were in full blossom, as far as the eyes could see, spread out in an extensive colourful garden. Also to be admired were scores of unusual flowers, unknown to the Asian world.

While in Germany, there were visits to Trier, Bonn and Cologne and several beautiful areas around the Eifel. There were also trips to Luxembourg and to Belgium. What made the most impression on Gyan Jyoti was the possibility of crossing borders in Europe without border posts, and without passport control.

Germany fascinated him, especially the groups of pilgrims he saw several times while driving through the Eifel. The groups were on foot on their way to Trier, where the Holy Vest of Christ was on display again – the last time it had been displayed to the public was in 1959. There were also groups going on their annual pilgrimage to Saint Matthias in Trier, the only Apostle of Christ buried on the northern side of the Alps.

At the Botanical Garden in Bonn, he was fortunate to see the giant, almost two meter high Titanic flower in full bloom. An unusual plant, which attracted thousands of German visitors, eager to see a single giant flower which flowered only once in every one to three years.

He travelled to France accompanied by his daughter and her husband, to meet Gendun Rinpoche. The last time that Gyan Jyoti had met Gendun Rinpoche was in Kalimpong in 1968, as he was by then spending more time for his business in Calcutta. It was after almost thirty years that they were meeting again, this time at the opposite end of the world, at the Kagyu Monastery in the little village of Le Bost, located in the Auvergne in France.

It was moving to see the happiness shown by Gendun Rinpoche to meet his benefactor again. Lama Pourtse had visited Gyan Jyoti in Kathmandu a few years earlier, but he was as much pleased as Gendun Rinpoche to see Gyan Jyoti finally in France. A framed photo of the Kalimpong 11th Mile house taken by Hans on his 1993 Kalimpong visit, was presented to Gendun Rinpoche. It was received with great pleasure, and for a long while he kept looking at the house, unable to take his eyes away.

The opportunity was taken to visit Lama Jigme at Dagpo Monastery, which lies halfway between Le Bost and Bordeaux. For the Asians, it is definitely almost the end of Europe.

At Le Bost, Gyan Jyoti was accommodated in the house reserved for the Karmapa at the request of Gendun Rinpoche, while his daughter and her husband were put up below Gendun Rinpoche's room. All the Lamas of the monastery went out of their way to see that Gyan Jyoti and his family were extended a comfortable stay for the few days they were there.

One day, while taking photos together outside the Karmapa house (today out of bounds to lay people) Gyan Jyoti holding Gendun Rinpoche's hands said to Hans: "The Karmapa gave me a precious stone and I never recognized it was a diamond."

Gyan Jyoti asked Gendun Rinpoche if there was anything he could do for him. Any help needed? Something still required for the temple under construction? Anything for Rinpoche himself? Gendun Rinpoche laughed. He had everything, and all was going well. If he remembered something that he would need, then he would not hesitate to ask.

At one of their last meetings, Gendun Rinpoche had a request. A complete set of the Kangyur and Tengyur manuscripts were needed for the monastery. He wished to have the manuscripts that were prepared in Tibet, and not in Nepal.

Back in Nepal, several inquiries were made before the manuscripts could be ordered from Tibet. It was no simple task, but they were finally transported to Kathmandu over the Khasa land route. The manuscripts were then given a last finishing touch by the Tibetan monks of Boudha, which took another few weeks. They had to be individually prepared with the traditional brocade slips before they were ready to be shipped to France.

The next problem was encountered at the Kathmandu airport, where the custom official wanted to see the bill. There was no bill. It took some time to get the papers organized, and to Gyan Jyoti's relief, this problem was also soon solved. The manuscripts were finally on their way to France.

The manuscripts weighed over seven hundred kilogram and were packed into eight boxes. Manoel Barbosa of Paris was contacted by the monastery, who then took charge of the consignment on its arrival at the airport in Paris.

Manoel remembers it was a full moon day when he drove to the monastery at Le Bost with the boxes loaded into his wagon. An auspicious day for the Buddhists, and an auspicious day for the holy manuscripts to be delivered to the monastery. The journey which normally took him four hours from Paris, now required ten hours.

Gendun Rinpoche was extremely happy to receive the good news that the Kangyur and Tengyur manuscripts had finally arrived at Le Bost.

Gendun Rinpoche died at the Le Bost Kagyu Monastery in the Auvergne on 31st October 1997. He left behind a firm

Buddhist establishment, dozens of Europeans who had become Buddhist monks and nuns, and hundreds of Europeans who had taken up Buddhism inspired by his teachings, and drawn by the unseen powers of his being, and his spiritual guidance. Deb Shova represented her father at the funeral ceremony at Le Bost, which was attended by hundreds of followers of Gendun Rinpoche.

Gyan Jyoti's next visit to France was in 1998 with Laxmi Prabha, again accompanied by his daughter and her husband in Germany. There were more visits. The last visit to France and Germany was in the late summer of 2002.

A couple of months before his last trip to Europe, Gyan Jyoti visited Rumtek. At the request of Shamar Rinpoche Gyan Jyoti had agreed to visit Rumtek Monastery to take an inventory of the Karmapa valuables and religious objects still remaining in the monastery.

He spent three days in Kalimpong with Shamar Rinpoche before travelling to Rumtek. Gyan Jyoti was not happy with what he saw. Security of the rooms was questionable, seals clearly appeared to be faked, and he was convinced that many genuine religious articles had already been removed.

During his last visit to Le Bost in France, he made it a point of going to Paris to meet the Seventeenth Karmapa who was there for a few days. There he gave the Karmapa a detailed report of the inventory, and his personal opinion of the whole incident.

A Helping Hand

In 1970 Gyan Jyoti travelled to Hong Kong for the first time, to participate in a World Buddhist Conference. While in Hong Kong, he looked up an old Chinese friend from his Kalimpong days. The friend invited him out to dinner, but first he had to take Gyan Jyoti shopping. Despite protests the friend argued that Gyan Jyoti should be wearing a western suit when travelling abroad, and not his regular *kameez sulwar* which looked out of place outside India. So Gyan Jyoti got his first and only western suit, complete with a couple of white shirts, a belt and a tie, and though he felt uneasy in the suit, it accompanied him the next few years in all his future Asian travels.

Gyan Jyoti then visited Japan in time for the Expo 70 in Osaka. He was shown around Japan, its beautiful Buddhist temples and lodgings for monks, by Sumangal Bhikkhu of Kathmandu. Gyan Jyoti's first thought was why such facilities could not be arranged in Kathmandu too, so foreign monks stopping over in Kathmandu on their journey to Lumbini would have a decent place to stay in. His thoughts were also shared by Sumangal Bhikkhu.

Two years later, Sumangal Bhikkhu returned to Kathmandu after completing his studies in Japan. He established a committee with Gyan Jyoti as its chairman, and circa 1973 to 1980 Buddha Vihar was built at Bhirkutimandap in Kathmandu, with facilities for accommodating visiting monks. The Vihar was in the care of Sumangal Bhikkhu until his untimely death in 1999.

Gyan Jyoti never had time for himself. On Saturdays, the only day of the week which is a holiday in Nepal, he was even busier. He was hardly at home on a Saturday. Family members often wondered at his energy. There would be regular Vihar meetings to attend, a function here, a ceremony there. To collect visiting monks at the airport, a delegation to see off, a function to co-ordinate with other committee members, and several other activities. Or if he was at home, there would be visitors from morning to evening, coming to him with new problems, more invitations, a new project to discuss, and always requests for donation. Some took advantage of his generosity, but these were exceptions.

He also spent his time visiting sick monks, and strongly recommended horlicks to all.

Sudarshan Bhikkhu who died a couple of years ago loved relating this story to everybody who cared to listen to him.

"I was one time seriously ill, and very weak. I thought I would die soon. Everybody thought I would die. Gyan Jyoti Sahu came to see me one day and he brought horlicks for me. He said I must drink horlicks and it would make me strong again. He told me about his sickness in Lhasa, and how it had saved him. Gyan Jyoti Sahu then personally fed me with warm horlicks, and everyday I felt I was getting stronger, and beginning to feel normal again. And here I am today, strong and well standing in front of you."

The International Meditation Centre was inaugurated at Sankhamuhl in 1986 and Gyan Jyoti as a founding member was elected committee chairman. He actively supported the centre, and for the maintenance of the place during its initial stage, had labourers and gardeners from his own house working there whenever required. He gave generously to finance its extension. A building still under construction is to house young women who wish to join the Theravada order. They will now have the possibility of studying in Kathmandu, instead of having to go to Burma, Thailand or Sri Lanka. The centre has for many years also been sponsoring young people travelling to one of the Buddhist countries, if they wished to study there to become a monk or nun.

From circa 1994, he was actively involved as committee member and sponsor of the Boudha Bridyashram of Banepa. He also supported the construction of the Bairochan Tirtha temple.

Gyan Jyoti was regularly at the Shakya Singh Vihar of Patan, which over the years received large sums of donation from him. He was involved in almost every Vihar in and around Kathmandu, and Vihars as far away as Tansen, Butwal and Dharan. Today it would be hard to single out a Buddhist Vihar that did not receive financial support from him.

His help did not end with the Theravadas. Tibetan monks, Tibetan Gumbhas, Newar priests, all were helped in the same manner, and the support to all was continued over months and years.

He funded the publication of religious books in the Newar and Nepali languages. Tibetan manuscripts were also published on behalf of requesting monasteries. Gyan Jyoti who had already given away millions for the cause of religion and culture, never stopped donating until the week before he died.

Gyan Jyoti received several commendations for his unfailing support to various activities, especially among the

Newars. On 14th May 2004 (1st Jestha 2061 BS), less than two months before he died, The Buddhist Study Society of the Department of Buddhisim of Tribhuvan University, organized a function at the Shanker Hotel in Kathmandu, to honour him with the title of an Agradharmanudata. The first bestowed on any Nepali, for being the greatest donor in modern times in the field of *Dhamma* – religion.

23rd June 2004 Gyan Jyoti succumbed to his battle against cancer, and died peacefully at a private clinic in Tripureswar.

For three days Gyan Jyoti's last remain was kept in the living room of his house, and for three days prayers were offered for him by the Theravada monks and nuns, the Tibetan monks, and the Newar priests. For three days, from the moment the news of his death spread around Kathmandu, until the day of his funeral, people poured into the house with khadas, bouquets of flower, or money according to the Tibetan custom, to say their final farewell.

Laxmi Prabha was so overwhelmed and moved by the large number of people turning up everyday, that she said to her elder daughter, "My tears have stopped falling seeing the great honour your father is receiving everyday since the day he died."

On the third day, the day of the funeral, a young Theravada monk took the initiative of getting a photo of Gyan Jyoti enlarged and over a hundred prints printed in the local press, along with a little pamphlet giving his short life story. The photos were carried as banners by many who took part in the funeral procession, and the blue pamphlet was distributed to all. Some organisations arrived with black banners, many with Buddhist flags, and all waited in the garden patiently to take part in the funeral procession.

According to Gyan Jyoti's wish expressed to Laxmi Prabha some weeks before his death, the funeral procession made a detour and went past the Janbahal temple and the old Kel Tole ancestral area, before heading for the Bishnumati river below Swoyambhu Temple, where he was cremated according to Newar tradition.

On the way to Lhasa

Gyan Jyoti on a mule, wrapped up against the cold Tibetan weather

A pause at the Nathula Pass

The Lhasa Newars

Sitting L to R: Triratnaman Tuladhar, President; Nepalese Consular General; Gyan Jyoti, Vice President
Standing L to R: Purnakazi Tamrakar, Kuldharma Tuladhar, Laxmi Jyoti Dhakwa, Maitriratna Tuladhar, Dharmabahadur Dhakwa, Chaityaratna Tuladhar, Tejratna Tuladhar, Ratnaman Singh Tuladhar

*L to R: Darbay Krishna Kansakar, Dev Jyoti Kansakar, Gyan Jyoti,
Hari Bahadur Shrestha, and Kalu Tamang (1948)*

Gyan Jyoti & Dev Jyoti with other Lhasa Newars

The waiting room of the Jyoti Brothers office at
Nepali Building, Kalimpong

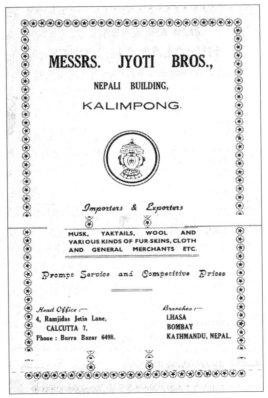

1950 Jyoti Brothers advertisement

200

On the occasion of Prof. Rahul Sankrityayan's birthday circa 1949, with the guests invited to a party organized by Gyan Jyoti at the Bhajuratna Kothi, 11th Mile, Kalimpong

L to R Sitting: 1) Sister of Queen Mother, present King of Bhutan's Aunt 2) wife of Bhutanese Prime Minister 3) Shakapa, Finance Minister of Tibet 4) Mahanam Bhante 5) Professor Rahul 6) Queen Mother, Rani Chuni Dorjee 7) Gyan Jyoti 8) Indian Professor for Sanskrit 9) Bhutanese Prime Minister, was assassinated some years later.

L to R Standing: 1) a Banja 2) Pasang Tempa 3) Lawyer Madam Babu Pradhan 4) Panda Tsang, a rich merchant of Tibet. Circa 1962 he was kidnapped by the Chinese while in Hong Kong, and has since then not been seen. 5) Lama Shakapa, brother of the Finance Minister 6) Sandu Tsang, a rich Tibetan merchant. His wife was the sister of Redding Lama. Died at the age of 40 in an accident while in Switzerland. 6) Professor for English from a University in Calcutta 8) Stenographer 9) & 10) Banjas

201

A group photo with Professor Rahul

Gyan Jyoti with Raja Dorjee of Bhutan, and Crown Prince Mahendra of Nepal in Kalimpong – 1952

Crown Prince Mahendra of Nepal

Crown Prince Mahendra in Kalimpong

Crown Prince Mahendra in Darjeeling

A Tea Party hosted in Darjeeling in honour of Crown Prince Mahendra

Gyan Jyoti – 1955

Younger brother Dev Jyoti

Gyan Jyoti – 1932

L to R: Gyan Jyoti's youngest sister Hera Shova, wife Laxmi Prabha, younger sister Gyan Shova and dog Renu

Family Photo – 1953

Family Photo – 1957

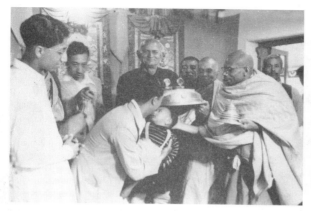

*Gyan Jyoti with
son Amrit Jyoti
when the
Sariputramaugalyan
relic was brought
to Kalimpong*

*L to R:
Dan Laxmi (Ratna
Jyoti's widow) and
Laxmi Prabha
Children:
Siddhi Laxmi,
Amrit Jyoti, Ganga
Shova, sitting
Deb Shova*

209

With the Dalai Lama

*With the Karmapa and
Dalai Lama's Guru*

*With the Karmapa's private secretary
Kon*

With Narad Bhikkhu

With the Panchen Lama in Calcutta

With the Dalai Lama in Kalimpong – 1957

Celebration of 2500th anniversary of Buddha Jyanti in Kalimpong in 1956

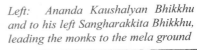

Left: Ananda Kaushalyan Bhikkhu and to his left Sangharakkita Bhikkhu, leading the monks to the mela ground

Scenes from the Buddha Jayanti celebration

Devotees going around the Dharmodaya Vihar shrine

Students of the Kalimpong Dharmodaya Hindi School

Dr. Roerich a well known Buddhist Scholar giving a speech

Gyan Jyoti at a function held at the Dharmodaya Sabha, Kalimpong.

The 16th Karmapa with Indian children in Siliguri

Amrit Jyoti, Shamar Rinpoche and Jigmela

Shamar Rinpoche with Laxmi Prabha

L to R: Kon's son, Amrit Jyoti, Jigmela and Shamar Rinpoche

The Bhajuratna Kothi at 11th Mile, with some parts of the garden, the lawn and some of the bee hives in the lower flat. Also seen in the picture above, is the half finished frame prepared for the bio-gas tank

218

Mr. Upendra Bahadur Basynet, Nepalese Counsular General to Tibet standing to the right, with the Jyoti children and his son Ashok Basynet who lived with Gyan Jyoti and his family for three years

L to R: Kon's son, Shamar Rinpoche, Amrit Jyoti, Jigmela, Dharma Shova and Deb Shova

The Jyoti children with Shamar Rinpoche's sister Chimey, who lived with the family for two years

The 16th Karmapa in the centre, with his monks during a visit to Kalimpong. Sitting second from right is Gendun Rinpoche

L to R: Second from left Kon, Kon's son, Shamar Rinpoche, Amrit Jyoti, Jigmela, Gyan Jyoti

Gendun Rinpoche with the three Tibetan monks who lived with Gyan Jyoti and his family at the 11th Mile in Kalimpong 1960–1972. Photos taken while on a Buddhist pilgrimage in India with the Jyoti family

Photo taken circa 1961 in New Delhi L to R: Mother-in-law Deb Prabha, wife Laxmi Prabha, sister Gyan Shova and the three children. Standing behind: Lama Sonam Pourtse and Gendun Rinpoche in the centre, and Tibetan servant Kapta to the far right.

At the Mahatma Gandhi Memorial in New Delhi

222

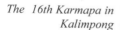
The 16th Karmapa in Kalimpong

Tibetan devotees waiting at the Bhajuratna Kothi to be blessed by the Sixteenth Karmapa during one of his visits to Kalimpong.

The 16th Karmapa in Kalimpong

The last meeting with the 16th Karmapa in Rumtek, in early 1981, just before the Karmapa's departure for America. Photo taken in the aviary.

The double storied building at the back, a part of the aviary which housed several birds

M/S Jyoti Brothers B.B. H. Mines
Photo taken on the occasion of the farewell party given to Mr. & Mrs. Gyan Jyoti
on 19.10.1963. Mines Manager C.V. George next to Hera Ratna Tuladhar the
Office Manager, Mrs. Hera Ratna Tuladhar, Laxmi Prabha, Gyan Jyoti. Others in
the photo are Supervisors, Foremen, Lorry Owners and mine workers.

A Jyoti Brothers
truck waiting to be
loaded, and a part
of the mining field

226

Photo taken in Kathmandu with Thervada nuns. Also seen in the picture is Gyan Jyoti's mother, sister Hera Shova and Dev Jyoti's wife Saraswati. Children from left: Amrit Shova, Padma Shova, Purna Jyoti, Uttam Shova

Gyan Jyoti in Japan with Sumangal Bhikkhu – 1970

Looking Back

The House in Kathmandu

Above L to R: Reshmi, Benu Shova, Anna, Surjya Kumari, Birjay Bahadur, Shanta Shova, Chandra Bahadur

With grandson Ajay

Front L to R: Nina, Ajay, Anand, Archana
Back L to R: Benu S, Siddharth, Shanta S.

The family –1971

Gyan Shova with Shanta S.

L to R:
Gyan S, Deb S,
Gyan Jyoti,
Laxmi Prabha,
Benu S, Shanta S,
son-in-law
Swoyambhu
Tuladhar and
Dharma S – 1978

Standing L to R:
Dharma S, Gyan S,
Deb S.
Sitting: Benu S. Laxmi
Prabha, Ajay,
Gyan Jyoti, Shanta S.

Relating travel tales to the grandchildren

Khicha puja day (dog's day) during the festival of Tihar
L to R: Benu S, Nina, Chimey, Laxmi Prabha

232

L to R:
Laxmi Prabha,
Benu S, Gyan Jyoti,
Dharma Shova and
Swoyambhu
Tuladhar

Bangkok L to R:
Shanta S, Anand,
Benu S, Ajay,
Archana, Nina,
and Siddharth

A holiday in
Bangkok with the
seven grandchildren
in December 1998.
L to R:
Benu S, Shanta S,
Anand Ratna,
Ajay Ratna, Laxmi
Prabha, Gyan Jyoti,
Archana, Siddharth,
Nina

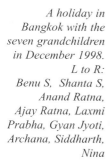

*With Gendun
Rinpoche, Lama
Pourtse and Hans
in France – 1996*

234

With Lama Jigme

L to R: Lama Djangchup, Hans, Lama Yeshi and Laxmi Prabha

With Drupla Choeing and Drupla Yongdrup – 2002

With Hans and Lama Tsony – 1996

L to R: with Anila Ridzin, Deb Shova, Laxmi Prabha, Lama Jigme and Lama Pourtse – 1998

Visits to Germany – enjoying the scenes and relaxing

237

A visit from Thervada monks of India

With Lama Doctor Paljor of Ladak, the present Dudjom Rinpoche's father-in-law. Meeting again after thirty years.

With Burmese guests in Kathmandu, standing to the left (above) is Dharam Das

239

At the end of the two day non stop Mahaparitran ceremony in the garden with Dharmapal Bhikkhu and Laxmi Prabha – Dec. 1999

Below: Guests at the Mahaparitran ceremony, the Thai Ambassador and the late Pavitra Bahadur Bajracharya of Patan

Bhajuratna Kothi at 11th Mile, Kalimpong. Home of the 17th Karmapa since September 1991

An inaugural ceremony

The Darjeeling Toy Train built 1881 is a passenger train which operated from Siliguri to Darjeeling.

Glossary

Unless otherwise stated, most words given below are Newari or integrated into the Newari vocabulary
(Nep.= Nepali; Hin.= Hindi; Tib.= Tibetan; Pali = Pali)

Anagarika	– a Theravada nun *(Pali)*
Anila	– a Tibetan nun *(Tib.)*
Avloktesvara	– the Buddhist goddess of mercy
babu	– boy
baidya	– a local doctor, or a person who knows the art of healing
baku	– a load
baniya	– a person who sells medical herbs
banja	– assistant
bhansachhen	– tax house
bhaucha pueygu	– blowing flames with the help of a bellow
Bhikkhu	– mendicant; a Theravada monk *(Pali)*
bhinapuja	– a Newari religious ceremony
bhojan daan	– donation of food
bhusya	– metal workshop
Bodhi Pipal	– the pipal tree under which Buddha meditated and gained enlightment
Buddha Jayanti	– the full moon day of Baishak, which falls in May, the day when Buddha was born, received enlightment and died.
chaitya	– another word for stupa which came into use to indicate the specific meaning of a shrine

Chakandyo	— another name for Singha Sartha Aju, who was the first to establish trade ties with Tibet. A Newari deity of Bhagban Bahal in Thabahil, today Thamel. On the day following the full moon of Falgun, which falls in March, it is taken in a procession to Asan and Indrachowk, to celebrate his historic return from Tibet.
champa	— roasted barley flour, also written as Tsampa *(Tib.)*
chapu	— scrap metal
chiriboka	— a sweet made from sugar
daan	— donation
dai	— elder brother
dal	— a lentil soup consumed with rice
darwan	— watchman *(Hin.)*
dema	— plate
Dasain	— the Hindu festival of Dushera *(Nep.)*
Dhamma	— religion
Diwali	— Hindu festival of light celebrated in honour of goddess Laxmi which falls around October / November *(Hin.)*
docha	— Tibetan high boots *(Tib.)*
doko	— a basket used for carrying goods by Nepali porters and farmers *(Nep.)*
doolie	— a palanquin, a covered litter *(Hin.)*
Dushera	— a Hindu festival going back to Indian mythology, to celebrate the conquest of the Hindu god Rama against the demon Ravana of Sri Lanka *(Hin.)*
gha	— a vessel used for carrying water
ghirling	— a ropeway system *(Nep.)*
gobar	— cow dung
gumbha	— a Tibetan monastery, also written gompha *(Tib.)*

gunla	– the tenth month in the Newar calendar which falls around August and is a holy month for Buddhist Newars
guthi	– an old tradition among the Newars it signifies an organization based on caste, kinship or locality, which ensures the continued observance of social and religious customs of the community
horlicks	– an instant malt product rich in vitamin and mineral, beneficial to the health and widely distributed in nearly every household; initially introduced into India by the British
hath bazar	– main market *(Hin.)*
jata	– horoscope
jinda	– follower, disciple *(Tib.)*
jyapu	– the farmer caste among the Newars
jyasachhen	– a workshop
kaan	– a semi bronze metal used by the Kansakars to produce their heavy plates and bowls
kaan dema	– heavy plates made of kaan
kaka	– younger uncle (paternal)
kaka baja	– grand uncle
kalas	– a vessel used for religious rites to hold consecrated water *(Hin.)*
kalighars	– hand workers, here copper and brass smiths *(Hin.)*
kameez sulwar	– shirt and trousers *(Hin.)*
kanya daan	– virgin offer *(Hin.)*
Karmapa	– The spiritual authority of the Karma Kagyu School and oldest Tulku line of Tibetan Buddhism. The line of incarnations of the Karmapa stretches over a period of nearly 900 years, from 1110 until today. *(Tib.)*

karuwa	— a small water vessel with a spout used for drinking water
Kasa	— a reference word for the Kansakars
kastu	— musk
kayta puja	— initiation ceremony for boys
khachara	— the offsprings of Newar men and Tibetan women.
khada	— auspicious white Tibetan silk scarves *(Tib.)*
khasi	— a large copper cauldron
khwasa	— a swearing word
Kotar	— a rich class of Tibetans *(Tib.)*
kothi	— house; shop; building *(Hin.)*
kumbah pyakhan	— a religious dance performed by the Newars at festivals
lakh	— a hundred thousand *(Hin.)*
lami	— a matchmaker, who arranges marriages between two families
Laxmi	— the Hindu goddess of wealth *(Hin.)*
Marwari	— ethnic Indians originally from Rajasthan, today a successful class of business people.
masta	— children
meet	— see *twae (Nep.)*
mela	— fair or festival *(Hin.)*
mohani	— Newari name for the Hindu festival of Dushera
momo	— steamed dumplings
momo bhara	— vessel for steaming the dumplings
nabaysal	— year ninety *(Hin.)*
Newars	— the original inhabitants of the Kathmandu Valley.
nikha	— morning prayers said with the help of prayer beads. The Newars will not eat in the morning without having said their *nikha*
paan	— beetle leaf chewed by Indians *(Hin.)*
paju	— maternal uncle

panchasheel	– the five buddhist vows *(Pali)*
paropkar	– social work *(Hin.)*
parsad	– religious offering *(Hin.)*
pataa	– a long white piece of cloth attached to the pinnacle of a stupa as a streamer dedicated to a deity.
paubha	– religious painting (a thanka)
puja	– a religious ceremony
puku	– child (*Tib.*)
pusabata	– large matching brass bowls
Ranas	– The aristocrat family in Nepal. In 1846 a young general Jung Bahadur Rana was appointed Prime Minister. He suppressed the power and authority of the King and made the prime ministership hereditary within his family. The Rana family ruled the country for 104 years until 1951.
Rinpoche	– an honorary term for a qualified and enlightened spiritual master *(Tib.)*
saa babu	– tastes good, boy
saga(n)	– a Newari rite applicable for all occasion, with the offering of whole boiled egg, whole dried fish and liquor.
sahu	– a rich man; a business man *(Hin.)*
satah	– an open building within or outside the city, left for charity. To be used for religious purposes or as a shelter
seto	– white (*Nep.*)
Sramaner	– non ordained Theravada monk (*Pali*)
stupa	– a domed building erected as a Buddhist shrine
Sunti	– Newari name for the Hindu festival of Diwali. It also marks the Newar New Year
Syamukapu	– white cap *(Tib.)*

taba	— father's elder brother
takachhen	— big house
tamang	— a special ethnic group in Nepal
tamdan	— a litter chair which is slung on a pole and carried by two men *(Nep.)*
tanga	— horse drawn cart *(Hin.)*
thachhen	— parent house
thakali	— a person chosen to manage an undertaking; the head or eldest of guthi, clan or family.
thanka	— religious painting *(Tib.)*
theba	— Tibetan load carriers *(Tib.)*
Theravada	— The teachings from the oldest of the order, also called the Pali school. The so called Pali canon was written in the 1st B.C. in Ceylon. It has a wide dissemination in Sri Lanka, Burma, Thailand, Cambodia and Laos *(Pali)*
Tihar	— Nepali word for the Hindu festival of Diwali, the festival of light when Laxmi the goddess of wealth is worshipped.
tinkha	brocade
tirtha yatra	— a pilgrimage *(Hin.)*
Tulku	— a reincarnated high lama and is given the same name as his predecessor *(Tib.)*
twae	— a ceremonial brother or sister relationship common among the Newars, to a non-related person.
vihar	— a Buddhist monastery and families (sangha) attached to the monastery
yelachingra	— another name for chiriboka

References

A Brief Report of the Kalimpong Dharmodaya Sabha, submitted to the 12th General Conference of the World Fellowship of Buddhist, held in Tokyo, Japan (1978), and the 17th General Conference in Seoul, Korea (1990)

Aryal, I.R. and Dhungyal, T.P., A New History of Nepal, Voice of Nepal (Pvt.) Ltd., 1975

Dagpo-Kagyu-Ling Program, June to September 1996, Centre for Study and Meditation

Donner, Dr. Wolf, Lebensraum Nepal, eine Etwicklungsgeographie, Institut für Asienkunde, 1996

Gellner, David N, Monk Householder and Tantric Priest, Foundation Books, New Delhi, 1993

Lall, Kesar, The Newar Merchants in Lhasa, Ratna Pustak Bhandar, 2001

Levy, Robert I, Mesocosm, Motilal Banarsidass Publishers, Delhi, 1992

Locke, John K. S.J., Karunamaya, The Cult of Avalokitesvara – Matsyendranath in the Valley of Nepal, Sahayogi Prakashan Kathmandu, 1980

Nepali, Gopal Singh, The Newars, an Ethno-Sociological Study of a Himalayan Community, Himalayan Bookseller Kathmandu, 1988 (reprinted from 1965)

Nepal Information, German-Nepal Friendship Association, Nr. 90, Dec. 2002

Thapa, Netra B. A Short History of Nepal, Ratna Pustak Bhandar, 1981

The Karmapa Papers, 1992

Tourist Guide to Kalimpong, A Travellers' Guide, Nest & Wings (India), Anand Prakash Agarwal, 1996

Tuladhar, Kamal, The Lhasa Newars, The Trans-Himalayan Traders, Shangri-La Royal Nepal Airlines inflight magazine, Vol 5. No. 1 January–March 1994

Tuladhar, Kamal, Caravan to Lhasa, Newar Merchants of Kathmandu in Traditional Tibet, Nepal Printing House, Kathmandu, 2004

Peissel, Michael, Tiger for Breakfast, Time Books International, New Delhi, 1966

Wangmo, Jamyang (Helly Pelaez Bozzi), The Lawudo Lama, Stories of Reincarnation from the Mount Everest Region, Vajra Publications Jyatha, Kathmandu, 2005

www.tourindia.com

www.kagyuoffice.org

www.tibet.com

www.simhas.org/karma16